The Triumph of Emotions

The Triumph of Emotions

Geopolitics in an Age of Resentment, Anger and Fear

DOMINIQUE MOÏSI

polity

First published in 2025 by Polity Press

Polity Press
65 Bridge Street
Cambridge CB2 1UR, UK

Polity Press
111 River Street
Hoboken, NJ 07030, USA

ISBN-13: 978-1-5095-5976-3

A catalogue record for this book is available from the British Library.

Library of Congress Control Number: 2024946644

Typeset in 11 on 13 pt Sabon
by Cheshire Typesetting Ltd, Cuddington, Cheshire
Printed and bound in Great Britain by CPI Group (UK) Ltd, Croydon

The publisher has used its best endeavours to ensure that the URLs for external websites referred to in this book are correct and active at the time of going to press. However, the publisher has no responsibility for the websites and can make no guarantee that a site will remain live or that the content is or will remain appropriate.

Every effort has been made to trace all copyright holders, but if any have been overlooked the publisher will be pleased to include any necessary credits in any subsequent reprint or edition.

For further information on Polity, visit our website:
politybooks.com

Contents

Introduction

In my book *The Geopolitics of Emotions: How Cultures of Fear, Humiliation and Hope Are Reshaping the World*, published in 2009, I attempted to draw a mapping of the emotions of the world. I was convinced that in order to understand our changing geopolitical environment, we had to decipher the leading emotions behind our cultural differences. I found more hope in Asia, following the economic growth of China and India. I perceived more humiliation in the Arab/Muslim world in the aftermath of the war in Iraq, and the second Intifada in Israel. And I saw more fear of the present and the future in the Western world, in both the United States and Europe.

There existed, of course, hard cases, countries that were not dominated by one emotion, but reflected a balance among them. For example, Russia, Iran, and Israel all displayed more than their share of fear, humiliation, and hope. The African continent oscillated between despair and hope, while Latin America navigated between demagogy and progress.

My ambition in this new book is to revisit the world through the same lenses, through the prism of emotions. I wish to explain how and why the problems I identified in *The Geopolitics of Emotion* have deepened and worsened. Why have emotions triumphed? In the concluding chapter of that 2009 book, "The World in 2025," I engaged in an exercise of historical fiction aimed at developing citizen reflexes. What would the world look like if fear were to come to dominate it, or, conversely, if hope were to rule?

Fear has prevailed over hope

We have now reached 2025. And the verdict of history is crystal clear: fear has prevailed over hope and the world today is much closer to the worst-case scenario that I had imagined than it is to the best-case vision I had dreamt of. I was realistic enough in 2009 to know that the hopeful scenario was just a dream, that could never really materialize. But I was idealistic enough to consider my Cassandra predictions as a wake-up call, a cautionary tale of a future doomed never to occur. And, to be fair, it did not. But with the return of war in Europe, the risks of an extension of war in the Middle East, the rise of nationalism and populism around the world, the retreat from globalization, the tragic acceleration of climate change, and the dark side of information technology revolutions, not to forget the immense potential consequences of AI (artificial intelligence), negative emotions have not only clearly triumphed over positive ones, they have also multiplied and diversified – some might be tempted to say they have exploded. To understand the world today, you have to add to humiliation and fear such raw emotions as anger and resentment, if not rage and even hatred. As a result, the new emotional order of the world is not only darker, as in the last paintings Van Gogh did at Auvers-sur-Oise in the months that preceded his suicide; it is also more complex, and much less defined by geography than was the case in 2009. And there have been major differences. In Asia for example, hope is far more manifest today in India than it is in China, with the rising demographic of the former in contrast to the slowing economy (and demographic) of the latter. With the explosion of Chinese nationalism in the region, if not in the world, an Asian West has emerged that is even more evident than it was in the early 2000s, encompassing countries such as Japan, South Korea, and Taiwan. These three countries may be geographically in Asia, but in strategic and emotional terms, they now perceive themselves as integral parts of the West. Their soft power is essentially Western. In the Middle East, hope is no longer confined to the confetti of history incarnated by the Emirati kingdoms. Under the heavy hand of Mohammed bin Salman (MBS), Saudi Arabia is experiencing a not-so-tranquil revolution toward modernity. Israel, on the other hand, while continuing to ignore the plight of the Palestinians – and paying, as we are just seeing, a very high price as a result – is confronted with the deepest identity crisis of its seventy-five years of existence.

One might be tempted to argue provocatively that, if looking for hope, it is more present in Europe, in a country like Ukraine – in spite of the terrible sufferings inflicted upon them by war – than it is in Asia in an empire such as China. Even among the ruins of their cities systematically destroyed by Russian bombs, Ukrainians, led by their charismatic Churchillian-like president Volodymyr Zelensky, remain convinced that, at the end of the day, if the West continues to support them, "David will prevail against Goliath." Russia's aggression crystalized their identity, leaving them with only one choice: to belong to the West. By contrast, one finds much less hope in China now than earlier in the century. Economic growth has fallen from above 10 percent to below 5 percent (if not much less, as the construction bankruptcies indicate). COVID-19 caused a collective trauma, and demographic realities have hit home. China is no longer the most populated country in the world.

Furthermore, emotions everywhere are far more "mixed" than they were in 2009. To attempt once more a daring

comparison between geopolitics and the world of impression-
ist paintings, colors have not only darkened, but have lost their
dominating tone. Darker shades of gray have progressively
replaced lighter ones, even if rays of light pierce through the
accumulation of clouds, or briefly replace the explosions of
thunder. In October 2023, elections in Poland and the return
to power of a pro-European and pro-democracy majority was
proof that illiberal democracy can be overcome. And that populism can be resisted and defeated. The leader of the party
of moderation and rationality, Donald Tusk, a former prime
minister in his own country and a former president of the
European Union, managed to mobilize huge crowds, under the
motto "Make Poland Decent Again." These were not his words,
but they reflected his message.

Between a bipolar and a tripolar world

These shifts in emotions have accompanied, if not created,
deep transformations in the international order (or disorder) of
the world. The bipolar order of the Cold War period (1947–89)
can be seen in retrospect as artificially simple. Two blocs were
facing each other, each one presided over by a single power,
the United States on the one hand, the Soviet Union on the
other. The two rivals were united by a common fear of nuclear
Armageddon, and an understanding of the rules of the balance
of terror. To quote French philosopher Raymond Aron, "peace
was impossible, war improbable." Nothing would of course
be more misguided than to idealize a period that came so
close to apocalypse in October 1962 during the Cuban missile
crisis. But the bipolar system of the Cold War period felt, and
probably was, much simpler than the multipolar balance of
power of Ancien Régime Europe. And the American unipolar
moment of the post-Cold War years (between 1991 and 2001,
from the fall of the Soviet Empire to the fall of the twin towers

in Manhattan) was so short, that it is difficult to derive valid lessons from it.

Today, against the backdrop of US/China rivalry, the war in Ukraine, and conflict in the Middle East, one can read the world in two different, yet not necessarily incompatible, ways. Some will see the return of a bipolar system, with China replacing the Soviet Union in what can be described as an updated version of the Cold War. To plagiarize an old saying, one could say: "It has the color of the Cold War, it has the smell of the Cold War, but it is not the Cold War." China is a global power, something the Soviet Union never was. And the world needs China, just as much as China needs the world. The Soviet Union was a unidimensional power, a pure object of fear, mostly just a nuisance value in the last decades of its existence. The socialist ideal did not long survive the crimes of Stalin as a source of hope. But what happens when China, your main rival, is also your main trading partner, when the geopolitical rivalry becomes a lose/lose game in the realm of geo-economics?

There is another reading of the world: one that looks especially relevant since the beginning of the war in Ukraine, and even more so since the start of the Israel/Hamas war in the Middle East, that could – if only in the short term – distract the United States from its legitimate fixation both with Asia, and also, to be more precise, with China. Can we say that, beyond the rivalry between China and the United States, a new tripolar order is emerging, between the Global South, the Global East, and the Global West? An order that reflects the new emotional balance of the world, featuring resentment and hope in the Global South, humiliation and anger in the Global East – clearly in Russia, but also in China though on a different scale – and fear and resilience in the Global West? In its very essence, this second reading of the world expresses an inescapable reality. In 1975, Chinwezu, a Nigerian writer educated in the United States, published a punchy essay called "The West and the rest of us." Today, it would be excessive to describe the Western world as an "endangered species" even if, in demographic terms, it represents little more than 10 percent of the world population. But the West has clearly lost the centrality and primacy it enjoyed for centuries. And "we" Westerners have to face this reality with a combination of humility for what we have become, and ambition and determination for the values for which we continue to stand. Robert Badinter, a former minister of justice for France and a towering European moral figure, said not long before his death: "It is not because our values are no longer consensual that they are not universal." In 2009, when I wrote *The Geopolitics of Emotion*, the Western world still enjoyed the illusion that it remained the center of the world. In his bestselling book *The Post-American World*, published in 2008, the American writer and journalist of Indian descent, Fareed Zakaria, announced the coming of a new power balance. But, for him, America was not in decline; it was the rest of the world, led by China and India, that was catching up with the United States. Today, the West has to face a harsh reality: it is only one of the centers of power and influence in the world; it has lost its monopoly as a model. The Chinese today (the Indians tomorrow?) are proposing alternative global models of political, social, and economic development. In cultural terms, the soft powers of countries such as South Korea and India are noticeably progressing, albeit with a mixture of imitation and competition with the West. In the world of fashion, the African continent has slowly made itself felt with the success of African-born designers, and the popularity of African materials, even in the world of *haute couture*. And in the world of sports, Saudi Arabia, thanks to its "deep pockets," is attracting some of the best soccer players in the world.

The world has never been more emotionally diverse precisely at the very moment it is faced with a poly-crisis. A multiplicity of actors and a multiplicity of challenges: an embarrassment of riches of the sort that can so easily lead to a perception or reality of chaos.

Globalization and interdependence

One should not confuse globalization and interdependence. The retreat from globalization may have begun in economic terms several years ago in 2007–8 with the financial and economic crisis: the fall of Lehman Brothers remains as the symbolic equivalent to the fall of the twin towers in Manhattan. But globalization has never been more present in cultural terms. And as far as economics and geopolitics are concerned, the world has become more interdependent. One used to say in the past that when America sneezed, the world caught a cold. The same could be said today of China. And it is hard to ignore the possible consequences of the war in Ukraine for the future of the South China sea. Will Russia's invasion encourage Beijing to apply force to gain control of Taiwan? Or will it, instead, instill in Chinese elites a sense of prudence that has been lacking since Xi Jinping came to power? The triumph of emotions in 2025 makes one think of geopolitical tectonic plates moving simultaneously in all directions and at an accelerated pace.

But the novelty of our world does not stop there. We must add two other dimensions if we are to understand the depth of the challenges we are collectively facing.

The first one can be described as follows. Geopolitics and politics, the international and domestic realms, are, so to speak, increasingly merging in ways that were unthinkable in 2009. What unites both realms is a common evolution toward emotional fragmentation and polarization. Alongside the multiple revolutions in the world of communication and information, international and domestic politics are negatively reinforcing each other through a process of disinformation and fake news. The United States is a perfect illustration of this

point. The West has not only lost its centrality and status with
the emergence of a much more complex and balanced world;
it has also seen a deep transformation of its image. The central
actor of the West, America, has moved from being a model to
becoming almost a counter-model. For the demonstrators of
Tiananmen Square in Beijing in May 1989, or much closer to
us in Hong Kong in the mid-2010s, the Statue of Liberty was
still a symbol of hope. The core message of Hollywood's golden
years, "if you can dream it, you can do it," expressed in such
diverse movies as *Working Girl* and *Schindler's List*, incarnated
a nearly universal dream. I still remember with the deepest of
emotions Frank Capra's 1930s movies: *Mr Deeds Goes to Town*
and, even more so, *Mr Smith Goes to Washington*. They were
powerful tributes, from an Italian-born director, to the greatness of American democracy during the years of Franklin D.
Roosevelt's presidency. The election of Donald Trump to the
US presidency in 2016, and in particular the attempted coup
represented by the march on the Capitol on January 6, 2021,
have increasingly been seen as a warning, a wake-up call for
Western and non-Western democracies alike, on the frailties
of their own political systems. It would be an exaggeration to
say that America has moved from being the pillar of stability
in the world (think of Vietnam, think of Iraq) to becoming
the main cause of its destabilization (think of Putin's Russia).
Nevertheless, the "shining city on the hill" is increasingly seen
as a prefiguration of everything that can go wrong in a democracy as it moves from being an external hyperpower to being a
domestically hyperpolarized society. As if these international
and internal complexities were not enough, what is radically
new in our present global context is that these geopolitical and
political changes are taking place in the shadow of two major
evolutions: climate change on the one hand, and AI on the
other. Climate change, with its unpredictable speed and depth,
makes the encounter between growing geopolitical rivalries
and political fragmentation nothing less than a suicidal and

gigantic distraction. Why claim a bigger part of the cake (think of Russia), if the cake itself (our planet) is in danger of disappearing? Or if the significant warming of growing regions of our planet makes them no longer habitable under the combined threat of extreme heat, fires, and flooding? How will richer countries deal with climate refugees?

As for AI, it might radically transform not only the nature of war, with drones replacing bombers, and robots eventually replacing soldiers, but, even more frightening, the nature of work and the meaning of life. Why should I live, if "I" can no longer make a difference for myself or for others? Or if it is not the economic crisis that deprives me of my job, but a technological revolution that renders me useless and obsolete? Of course, to be fair, there is a much more positive and humanistic reading of the impact of AI, from its revolutionary use in the world of medicine to its positive impact on the economy and society.

But of all the factors that have changed or simply revealed the new emotional order of the world, the most significant – for Europeans at least – has been the return of war on our continent, barely eighty years after the end of World War II, and taking place at little more than a two-hour flight from Paris.

This is the reason why *The Triumph of Emotions* will begin with an assessment of the emotional consequences for the world of the war in Ukraine. For this war has accelerated, if not revealed, the emergence of a new emotional divorce in the world.

October 7, 2023 has been sometimes described as the "September 11" of Israel. It may represent something even more significant for the Jewish state. The bloodiest pogrom since the end of World War II questions the Israeli state's very purpose: the protection of Jews in the world in the aftermath of the Shoah. This act of barbarism in the Middle East, followed by an excessive and ill-advised response on the part of the Israelis, confirms the very thesis of this book concerning the growing weight of emotions in the world. And it echoes the dual thesis I was defending in *The Geopolitics of Emotion* where I presented the conflict between Israelis and Palestinians not only as the "tragic matrix" of the international system, but as the "archetypal encounter between two primary emotions: humiliation and fear." A nation has been born out of a unique and absolute tragedy. A people has been crushed and oppressed by a victim rendered blind to the suffering of the "other" and by the immensity of its own physical and psychological wounds.

A leading member of the Palestinian elite once memorably described to me how his people felt: "It is as if you were walking in the streets of the city where you were born and suddenly, above your head, a window opens and someone throws out of that window a human being that crushes you as he touches the ground. The unfortunate passer-by is of course the Palestinian; the person responsible for the defenestration is the European; and his victim, who in turn becomes the oppressor of the Palestinian, is the Israeli Jew." And he concluded: "Nothing could be more emotional than this tragic encounter taking place on the world stage still dominated by the conflicting guilt of a Western European world torn between the memories of antisemitism and colonialism." The problem for Israel is that, with the process of time, the first memory (antisemitism) has slowly but irresistibly faded, while the second one (colonialism) has resurfaced with a vengeance. Israel, of course, and particularly its present political leadership, bears a heavy responsibility for this process. It is as if the nationalism of the land, in the manner of a magnifying glass, was emphasizing the "sins" of the victim, to the detriment of the memory of the immensity of his sufferings; and, in the process, was neglecting to mention the exceptional character of his feats, scientific, technological, as well as cultural.

At the emotional level, the consequences – international as well as domestic – of what can be described as Israel's fifth war easily turn out to be huge, not only for the state of Israel and the Middle East at large, but also for the Jewish people. Israel was their ultimate protection, if not their life insurance. Could it become a source of vulnerability, even an objective danger?

1

War in Ukraine and the Emotional Divorce of the World

War as a game changer

As a baby-boomer, born in France in 1946, right after the end of World War II, I belong to a generation that has never been directly confronted with war. I was too young to serve in the Algerian War and I feel privileged to have escaped the major tragedies of life. It was as if my status as the son of an Auschwitz survivor and the incommensurable sufferings experienced by my father had given me some kind of special protection, if not immunity. (I am of course speaking here as a West European.)

But in the early morning of February 24, 2022, I felt keenly as if the long post-World War II parenthesis of peace had ended. It was as if, after being accustomed to eating the biblical "white bread," during the first seventy-five years of my life, the time for "black bread" had brutally come. I am fully aware that French psychoanalyst Boris Cyrulnik, who has worked on the concept of resilience, was much more disturbed than I was on that morning. He had miraculously survived World War II and Nazi persecution. Suddenly, long-forgotten or suppressed images and sounds of his youth were resurrected and coming back to haunt him. War was back in Europe. Privileged by my postwar birth status, I had been presumptuous enough to believe that I could and would escape the tragic nature of history. "The Gods" had punished me. But history was catching up with my generation. Of course, I do not forget that, just thirty years earlier, war had already returned to Europe, in the Balkans, following the collapse of the Soviet Union and the disintegration of Tito's Yugoslavia. But those wars, even though tragic in their own right, never threatened the stability of the world or even the core of Europe. No one ever spoke of the risks of a Third World War and/or of the possible use of nuclear weapons. And the number of casualties in ex-Yugoslavia over nearly a decade did not begin to reach the level of casualties caused by the war in Ukraine in three years (at the time or writing, already more than 200,000).

On the morning of February 24, I felt like an analyst reinforced in the validity of my judgment or, more probably, of my intuition on emotions. I had simply taken at face value the analysis and predictions of the CIA that sounded so plausible and had announced the inevitability of war. It was foolish not to take them seriously. All the signs were there, written on the wall. I still remember a very distinguished member of the French Academy asserting with an air of absolute certainty, just a few days before the first Russian invasion: "Putin will not go to war, he is not stupid." But if I was reassured as an analyst, I was appalled as a citizen by the tragic absurdity of the event. Confronted with existential challenges such as climate change, or the return of pandemics like COVID-19, an epidemic we were only just beginning to surmount, we should all have felt ourselves to be "in the same boat." But in strategic and emotional terms, that was clearly not the case.

As I write these lines, the war in Ukraine is still unfolding. All outcomes are possible, from a Russian victory to some kind of stalemate leading to an indeterminate and possibly indefinite truce, like in Korea. But whatever its conclusion, this war will remain a global game changer in geopolitical, if not economic, political, and even cultural terms. Above all, in the field of emotions, the return of war to Europe has both revealed and accelerated the emotional divorce of the world. The war not only separates Europeans from non-Europeans, but also Europeans among themselves, for Russians are also European. It also distinguishes Westerners among themselves, while potentially pitting Americans against Europeans.

Tell me what you think of the war; I will tell you who you are

The war in Ukraine reveals, above all, the emotional divorce that exists between Westerners and non-Westerners. Empathy for the plight of Ukrainians is a product not only of geography and history, but also of political culture. The more democratic your country is, the easier it is for you to relate to the sufferings of the Ukrainians, and to perceive the danger of Russian expansionist adventurism. From this standpoint, Central Europeans rely more on the West's responses than ever. They not only feel geographically close to Ukraine, they still have in their genes – even indirectly for those born after 1989 – the experience of Soviet occupation. Seeing Russian tanks rushing to seize control of Kyiv evoked for a majority of Central Europeans memories of Budapest in 1956, or Prague in 1968. A "kidnapped Europe" – to use Milan Kundera's apt and vivid formula – could only "feel" for the Ukrainians. Beyond empathy and a sense of shared destiny, there was also undiluted fear in the Baltic Republics, which were part of the Soviet Union until 1991, as well as in Poland. Poles may have retained in a tiny part of their collective memory a souvenir of their short occupation of Moscow in 1610. They remember much more clearly the three successive divisions of their country between 1772 and 1795 by the Russian and Austrian Empires and the

Prussian kingdom; or, more recently, in 1944, the Soviet Army waiting on the other side of the Vistula River during the crushing of the Warsaw insurrection before intervening decisively to take control of the city. Not to mention the Katyn massacres of Polish elites attributed initially to Nazi Germany by the Soviet Army, but, in reality, committed under Stalin's orders at the outset of the war.

Memories that affect your mind do not necessarily have to be negative. The United Kingdom is a case in point. In the immediate aftermath of the Russian invasion of Ukraine, the images of destroyed Ukrainian cities, of civilians taking refuge in Kyiv's metro stations, seemed like a replay of the British "finest hour" in 1940, when they were alone in resisting Hitler after France's collapse, and before the entry of the United States into the conflict. The resistance, and the resilience of the Ukrainians, spoke to the deepest of British emotions, and Zelensky gradually came to be seen as a latter-day Churchill. By empathizing with the Ukrainians initially – more so than other Europeans (with the exception of Russia's own immediate European neighbors) – the British were engaging in a self-congratulatory emotional trip back to their own glorious past, when they successfully stood up to a superior Nazi Germany, and when, to quote Churchill, so much was "owed by so many to so few," to men who literally changed the course of history in May/June 1940.

France and Germany may yet lament the evolution of their privileged bilateral relationship. What happened to this Franco-German duo? The days of de Gaulle/Adenauer, d'Estaing/Schmidt, Mitterrand/Kohl seem far away. Sarkozy and Hollande pretended to have a close, excellent relationship with Angela Merkel, but this was not the reality. Macron and Scholz do not even try to hide the fact that theirs is a distant (at the least) relationship. The two countries, the two societies, have gone their own respective ways. But on the war in Ukraine, Germany and France have ultimately followed similar paths even if for different reasons and at a slightly different pace. Initially neither Paris nor Berlin believed in the ineluctability of the coming of war. And when it finally came, their initial reactions were of "moderation." In Germany, a combination of economic interest (if not greed) and historical remorse explained the willingness to keep the bridges open with Moscow beyond the reasonable and the acceptable. Germany had delegated its security to the United States, while the country's energy resources depended on Russia in an irresponsible way, all the more so since the abandonment of nuclear energy. And Russia was a prominent client of German industry. Pro-Russian economic lobbies were particularly active in the Federal Republic. But beyond greed, there was also remorse. Could Germany deliver Leopard II tanks to Ukraine eighty years after Panzer divisions had invaded Russia, inflicting so much damage and so many casualties to the Soviet people? Those who believed that the past continued to dictate the need for redemption were in a minority. Few Germans felt at the outset that even though German tanks had been an instrument of tyranny in the past, they should become part of the vehicle for freedom on the side of the Ukrainians today.

On the French side, a combination of excessive pride and some elements of naivety prevailed, starting at the Elysée Palace (the seat of the French presidency). Too confident in his charm and intellectual superiority, President Emmanuel Macron thought it was important to keep the dialogue open with Russia, arguing that "One should not humiliate Russia" – an argument that did not make sense. It was Russia that humiliated itself and not the West. Such a predicament also ignored the personality of Putin and the true nature of the Russian regime. France's willingness to remain a bridge between Russia and the West was of course based in part on an oversimplified interpretation of the Gaullist heritage and the existence of lingering elements of anti-Americanism favored by both the extreme right and the extreme left.

But Russian exactions in the field forced France and Germany to shift their positions and adopt stances on the war in Ukraine that were much closer to those of Central, Eastern, and Nordic Europe, not to mention the UK and the United States. Coverage of the war might be different in the UK, Germany, and France – the British more optimistic in general about the advances of the Ukrainian army, the German much more pessimistic, and the French in between – but in all three countries empathy with Ukrainians and condemnation of Russian war crimes became stronger with the process of time. Germany doubled its defense budget, entering into a new era on the military front, while on the energy front it managed to find substitutes for Russian resources (albeit in a non-ecological way through the use of coal). As for France, the country had to adjust to reality and accept the fact that it could expect nothing from Putin's Russia: Paris had to fall in line with the rest of Europe. And it even went further when President Macron suggested in the winter of 2024 "that one could not exclude Western troops on the ground." This toughening of France's position was a logical answer to Putin's escalation in deeds and in words. It also came after the coming to power of the extreme right in our southern neighbor Italy, which did not lead to any sort of rapprochement with Russia. Under the pragmatic and strong leadership of Giorgia Meloni, Italy has maintained a clear pro-Ukraine, pro-NATO, and pro-Europe position. The only dissenting voices in Europe have been heard in Hungary, Serbia, and Slovakia, three countries deeply split between pro-liberal, pro-European, pro-Western forces, and pro-Russian, anti-liberal forces. It is only natural that a pro-Slav tendency should be present in Serbia. The memory of the NATO bombings over Belgrade in 1999 constitutes a strong pro-Moscow argument. But at some point, Serbs will have to choose between their nostalgia for the past and the project for their future, a future that can only be in Europe, within the European Union, and more globally in the West. The case of

Hungary is different. Under the leadership of Victor Orbán, Europe's model for illiberal democrats is navigating shrewdly between defending its difference in the name of vital national interests and the need not to break away from the two organizations of which the country is a member: the European Union and NATO. But even Orbán's grip on power is becoming fragile with the process of time and, as in the case of Poland's ultra-conservative coalition, will come to an end.

In this European smorgasbord one should not forget a key actor, the European Union itself. Moscow was convinced Brussels would fail the test of the war in Ukraine. On that topic as well, Putin proved deeply wrong. In less than six months – through a combination of empathy for the Ukrainians, fear of Russia, and also lingering doubts about the long-term credibility of US protection – the EU did more for its security than in the three decades since the fall of the Berlin Wall. The prospect of being hanged in the morning concentrates the mind, as the British philosopher and polemicist Samuel Johnson used to say. Putin's wake-up call did not suppress the differences existing between those who gave priority to the strategic autonomy of Europe behind Macron's France, and those for whom the only answer was "more America." Europeans were taking different paths, but were nevertheless moving in the right collective direction. The case of NATO is even more spectacular than the case of the EU. Emmanuel Macron had previously declared NATO to be "brain dead." Unlike the Sleeping Beauty, she was not awoken by a kiss, but by a sudden blow and the sound of Russian tanks marching on Kyiv. Putin wanted to Finlandize Ukraine; what he got was an "Otanization" of Finland and a Sweden that abandoned its centuries-old neutrality to apply for NATO membership. The result: thanks to Putin, the Baltic Sea is about to become an Atlantic Lake.

The case of the United States is at the same time both clearer and more complex. From the beginning of the war in Ukraine, Biden's America was a key supporter of Kyiv, by far its most generous provider of military and economic help. Without America, or with a different (Republican?) America, Putin's plan may have succeeded. At the same time, one can only regret the delayed generosity of the United States. Had longer-range missiles or F16 fighter planes been delivered earlier, Ukrainian counteroffensives would have been more decisive and Ukraine would surely have reconquered more (if not most) of its lost territories – and would not have been losing them after the failure of its counteroffensive. Should one see in this American hesitation to make the right choice at the right time in Ukraine a replay of the late entrance of the United States in World War I and World War II? And could the long-delayed aid voted by the Congress in April 2024 be the equivalent for Ukraine of the entrance of America in April 1917 for the Allied Powers?

The answer is not so simple. In 2025, America is faced with another challenge, which takes priority: China. And although a majority of Americans (Democrats more than Republicans) are behind the Ukrainian cause, America is sufficiently at war with itself to hesitate to add an international war to what is becoming a civil one. And this, especially after the dubious successes of America's last military adventures in the Middle East. Joe Biden was not that much younger or more energetic than Andrew Jackson, president from 1829 to 1837, who united the country in the original version of America First, or the more cerebrally interventionist Theodore Roosevelt, president from 1901 to 1909, whose interventionist stances seemed a replica of European imperialism. But he is a true old-style internationalist, keenly aware of the deep divisions existing in his country. And in a pre-election year, he did not want to reinforce the chances of his Republican rival by overdoing it on the topic of Ukraine.

War is for "others"

All Europeans, aside from their differences, were startled by the return of war on their continent. We had all tended to believe in the powerful mantra of "Never Again," which, after World War II, seemed to float over our heads as a great protective roof. Europeans had given enough to war between 1914 and 1945. From now on, if war occurred, it would be for others. That at least was what we were convinced of, in our spontaneously progressive vision of history. With the process of time, the "Never Again" mantra has given way to a more restricted, some would say more selfish, ambition: "Never Again for Us" ("Us" meaning white, civilized Europeans, if not, more globally, Westerners). But past sufferings do not automatically protect you from new ones. The reverse can be true. Time not only heals, but can also aggravate memorial wounds. The result is a vendetta-like logic that can take over ever larger parts of the world. For in international terms, tragic memories and emotions, unlike skin, do not necessarily heal.

At the end of his book *The Committed Observer*, published in French in 1981, Raymond Aron remarked that "the events of the war [he meant the Shoah] progressively plunged into me. They signify more for me today than in 1945 or 1946." "This is paradoxical, but this is the way it is." Unfortunately, recent experiences demonstrate the complexity of time's "work." Think of America: more than fifteen years after the first election of a Black president, not only has the wall of skin color not fallen, but racially motivated crimes have never been so numerous. Think of the Middle East: resentment for the past has grown exponentially with the competing memories of the Shoah on the Israeli side and of the Nakba on the Palestinian side looming ever larger. Like abused children, Israelis are particularly insensitive to the plight of Palestinians. Their natural tendency would be to ignore them, the way rich citizens in Brazil or India do not see their transparently poor neighbors.

The Palestinians have become, to put it bluntly, a problem you cánnot solve and therefore a problem you wish to ignore. On October 7, 2023, the Palestinian question – as was the intention of the Hamas movement, which has governed Gaza since 2007 – returned in the most tragic and barbaric manner. It could only be perceived as a new pogrom by Israelis and Jews. But for the Arab/Muslim world, and more globally for the countries of the South, the war in Gaza has been the ultimate proof of the selective emotions of the Western world. Half a million deaths in Syria, at least 300,00 in Yemen, 200,000 in Sudan. But only 1,200 Jews on October 7! And the Western world is moving from indifference to passion. It is fair to say that, with the process of time and the growing number of Palestinian deaths (forty times more numerous than the figure of Israeli deaths at the time of this writing), emotions have shifted. The atrocious crimes committed by Hamas have quickly been superseded by the plight of the suffering population of Gaza. It was inevitable given the disproportionate use of force demonstrated by the Israeli forces. Their comparative advantage was in the field of selective elimination of their adversaries. But instead of repeating their treatment of the terrorists responsible for the attack on the Israeli athletes during the 1972 Munich Olympic Games, Jerusalem chose the heavy hand of Dresden- or Coventry-like bombings of World War II. Israelis are not only Jews in the eyes of the world; they are Westerners. While October 7 brings back memories to the Jewish world of the Warsaw Ghetto, it evokes echoes of the Algerian War (1954–62) for countries of the South. The former see Hamas's terrorists as Nazis, the latter as inheritors of the FLN (the National Liberation Front) in Algeria, whose members used terror to make their point and convince the French colonists to leave.

The problem is that, with time, the ruins of Gaza increasingly resemble those of the destruction of Warsaw, and the images of Palestinian children begging for food evoked memories of the Jewish children in the Warsaw Ghetto. This clash of emotions not only translates into a divorce between cultures, it has also created a generational divide within the Western world. The older you are, the easier it is to relate to the sufferings of the Jewish/Israeli people. Younger generations identify mostly with the suffering of the Palestinians. They have no way to balance the images of the present with those of the past.

As for the African continent, the scars of the imperial/colonial epoch seem to deepen with time. The recent antipathy and rage against France in the Sahel region in Africa (largely orchestrated by Moscow) is a case in point.

"Life must go on" was my father's motto after he survived Auschwitz and went on to support Franco-German reconciliation. This is clearly not today's dominating philosophy. "Silence like a cancer grows," Simon and Garfunkel sang in the 1960s. In our current world, it is not silence that grows, but anger and resentment, denunciation and intolerance. As if, with the distancing of time, one can no longer understand all the previous efforts made in the past to rebuild the present and construct the future, in spite of previous suffering. The spirit of reconciliation that once dominated the thinking of some of the most traumatized parts of the world (from the Franco-German model to South Africa's Rainbow Nation) has been replaced by a spirit of retribution. Justice must prevail at all cost, even if it means that rapprochement is put off to some distant future. Even if it means there will be greater darkness at the end of the tunnel.

The war in Ukraine can be seen as confirmation of this pessimistic vision of the process of time. We live in a world where past wounds appear more acute than they were decades ago, as resentment grows, rather than diminishes, with time. As if frustration with the present and fear for the future had made reconciliation with the past more impossible than ever.

For the rest of the world, the return of war in Europe is, at the same time, a serious and destabilizing challenge, with its economic and social but also international consequences. The war in Yemen, one of the worst humanitarian crises of the last decades, barely existed on the map of public opinion interest. Now, with war in Europe, that "distant" war has almost disappeared off the radar of international news – until it returned because one of the parties to the conflict, the Houthis, members of the Iranian-led "axis of resistance," which should be more accurately described as "axis of chaos," was incited by Tehran to acts of piracy designed to pressurize the international community. But the world does not care for Yemen; it cares for what the Yemen war may entail for international trade.

The war in Ukraine does not reveal only the selective emotions of the West, but also the selective emotions of the South. For the South, it is mostly a war among white Europeans. Very few countries of the South – with the notable exception of those included in the Asian West, such as Japan and South Korea – identify with the ideological, even less the ethical, nature of the conflict. Seen from the West, the war in Ukraine is the most Manichean the world witnessed since the American Civil War and World War II. It opposes the forces of "good," Ukraine, and the forces of "evil," Russia. Across the vast majority of Europe, pro-Ukrainian emotions still run deep, even if one does sense the start of a "Ukraine fatigue" in the face of the indirect impact of the strategy of fear pursued by Putin. Many Europeans, and even more Americans, surely ask themselves: "Do I really want to die for Ukraine, in what can so easily become World War III?"

For the poorer countries of the world, the war in Ukraine in terms of "good versus evil" is of little concern to them. Instead, it is they who are the most affected by the rise in the price of wheat and grain; they feel that, once more, they have been taken hostage by the power games of selfish "white men." In the first half of the twentieth century, they served as cannon fodder in two world wars. Now, they risk being starved to death by a combination of climate change and the continuous cynicism of power politics.

Between apprehension, indifference, and *Schadenfreude*; or how the Global South faces the war in Ukraine

For the non-Western world, the dominating emotions are drastically different from those of the West. One senses in them a combination of apprehension for the consequences of the conflict. But there is also a mixture of indifference, with some secret satisfaction (the German expression *Schadenfreude* conveys their feelings very well). As long as the war is contained and does not destroy the world economy, it can be seen as a form of retribution and even punishment for the Western world – retribution for past sins, starting with slavery, the crime of all crimes. Like a boomerang, the motto "Never again for us" has caught up with its creators. "You thought man-made folly and its culmination, war, had become the monopoly of non-Western countries? How complacent, how arrogant, how wrong you were!" This emotional reaction is also mixed with a more rational calculus. A war at the very heart of Europe, in which the United States is deeply involved, could be seen as a blessing for the most ambitious parts of the non-Western world. (This is what happened to Latin and Central America during World War II, when La Havana and Buenos Aires had become places of refuge, a sanctuary of cultures, places of creativity for all the emigrants, many of them Jews from Europe.) Today, this war among Europeans can only confirm and accelerate the passage of the torch of history from the Western to the Asian world. In their refusal to choose between the aggressed and the aggressor, leaders of the Global South have been greatly helped by Russian propaganda and what can be described as the triumph of the empire of lies.

"Propaganda is something very simple." This is what Jean Anouilh, a French writer of the first half of the twentieth century, used to say. "You simply have to say something very gross and keep repeating it very often." Putin, who presents himself in Russia as the heir of Peter the Great, though his reign resembles increasingly that of Ivan the Terrible, is greatly benefiting from the inheritance and image of the Soviet Union in the non-Western world. Such a policy is working from Africa to Latin America, and also in some parts of Asia and the Middle East from Syria to Iran. "During the Cold War, i.e., not that long ago, was I not on your side, against the imperialist camp?"

The sources of Putin's conduct

"The sources of Soviet conduct" was the title of a groundbreaking article published in 1947 by the journal of the New York Council on Foreign Relations, *Foreign Affairs*. The article was signed "Mr. X." The identity of the author was revealed later. He was a prominent American diplomat, a Russian and Soviet Union specialist, by the name of George Kennan. His analysis and recommendations served as the backbone of America's successful containment policy during the entire period of the Cold War. Kennan understood before anyone else that time was the essence of America's needed strategy. Washington had to contain Moscow as long as it took, and Moscow would collapse in on itself, victim of the structural contradictions of its system, between the strength of its military machine and the weaknesses of all the rest, starting with the economy.

What we need today is as sharp an analysis of "the sources of Putin's Russia conduct." What are the reasons that led him to invade Ukraine? What was his ultimate goal in doing so? How could he have been so wrong in his estimate of Russia's strengths and Ukraine's weaknesses? What was the role played by emotions in Putin's decision-making? In 2023, the former

CEO of Google, Eric Schmidt, wrote provocatively in an article published in *Foreign Affairs*, "Why technology will define the future of geopolitics," that if Russia had been led by AI instead of by Putin, Moscow would never have invaded Ukraine. The new technological breakthrough would have come to the conclusion that the risks of invasion were too great and the benefits too uncertain. But to reach the conclusion – which may still be proven wrong: the history of the war is far from written – that AI is superior to the emotional intelligence of Russia's new tsar is not enough. We have to ask ourselves what Putin's ultimate motives were in taking this fateful decision.

Ukraine and Putin

Should one emphasize, above all, the encounter between a specific territory (Ukraine), a particular leader (Putin), and a unique context, both international and domestic? And ask whether Putin wanted, at the same time, to exploit the perceived weaknesses of the West and to hide the growing economic if not political difficulties of Russia?

Let us start with the territory itself. Ukraine's status has always been extremely complex, and its history – you only have to read Serhii Plokhy's books – is one of the most tortuous you can think of, having been dominated at different times by Russia and Poland, not to mention Lithuania. I can personally bear testimony to this complexity. My grandfather on my mother's side, David Tabakman, was born in Odessa at the end of the nineteenth century. For most of my life, I considered myself to be of Russian (albeit Jewish) origins. These roots allowed me, in my various encounters and debates with my Soviet and then Russian professional colleagues, to repeat the same discourse: "I love Russian culture, but I am saddened by Russia's political culture. I know in my upbringing what I owe to Tolstoy and Chekov, not to mention Tchaikovsky or Shostakovich. I include these names in my beloved multiple

European identities." Yet at 4:55 a.m. on February 24, 2022, I started to think very differently about my identity: I was of Ukrainian descent and, to boot, certainly, a very distant cousin of Volodymyr Zelensky. My identity transformation became traumatic for my closest Russian friends. All the more so because some of them had difficulty coming to terms with Ukraine's independence after the disintegration of the Soviet Union. They could accept the independence of the Baltic Republics or Georgia, but Ukraine, the Little Russia (the title of Tchaikovsky's Second Symphony), Kyiv – it was simply a bit too much for them. They were fighting for democracy and the rule of law in Russia, but on the subject of Ukraine their deepest feelings were not so very different from those expressed by Putin. Ukraine was an artificial entity. They were neither dismayed nor surprised when I reported to them the story I had heard when I was teaching at the College of Europe in Natolin (close to Warsaw). According to my Polish friends, a very private conversation had taken place between Vladimir Putin and Donald Tusk at a time (around 2010) when the two men were prime ministers of their respective countries, Russia and Poland. They were speaking in German, without interpreters, and their exchanges went as follows (according, at least, to the report I got from my Polish sources). Putin, emphasizing the artificiality of Ukraine as an independent nation, is supposed to have made the following proposal to his Polish counterpart: "Let us divide Ukraine. I will give you the western part around Lvov, and I will take the rest." The problem is that this was not being proposed at the end of the eighteenth or at the beginning of the nineteenth century, but in the first quarter of the twenty-first century. Putin is said to have read many history books during his period of COVID isolation. Visibly, he had not then taken on board the fact that Poles were the last people to feel at ease with the form of brutal cynicism he offered them. Between 1772 and 1795, their country had been divided three times by their ambitious and greedy neighbors, and then again in 1939. Could they have treated Ukraine the way they had been treated themselves? The answer may have been "Yes" yesterday. But now they were a proud member of a democratic club: the European Union. Such a drastic "enlargement of Polish territory" simply did not make sense to them. It would have violated international law and the rules of the Union.

What is interesting in this real or invented story – it might have been a serious joke, a testing ground for Putin – is that it sounds so plausible. In fact, Belarus's President Lukashenko accused the Ukrainians during the summer of 2023 of preparing themselves to cede part of their territories – which he, of course, said did not belong to them, but to Russia – to Poland. Playing with ultra-nationalism is obviously a very old trick.

It also reminds us historically that, in his appetite for territorial expansion, Napoleon was the inheritor of Ancien Régime Europe; whereas Putin, in his emphasis on Russian history, presents himself in the particular case of Ukraine as the heir of Catherine the Great.

How do you deal with a despot whose only advisors are Ivan the Terrible, Peter the Great, and Catherine the Great? This remark has been attributed to Putin's foreign minister Sergei Lavrov. Was he complaining ironically about his fate, or simply admiring the depth and historical gravitas of his boss?

Shortly after he came to power, Putin famously said, and repeated many times, that the worst tragedy of the twentieth century had been the disappearance of the Soviet Empire. He could have mentioned Verdun, Auschwitz, or Hiroshima. He did not. His focus was on his Empire.

Putin's dual heritage

Over the course of time, Putin, like a musician writing variations on a theme, has chosen to present himself, in turn, as the descendant of the Russian Empire, the inheritor of the Soviet

Union, or simultaneously both. The newly elected Putin wanted to maintain a balance between both traditions. "Late Putin" is presenting himself increasingly as the last tsar of imperial Russia, rather than as the inheritor of the Soviet Union. The day after Yevgeny Prigozhin (the leader of the Wagner militia) attempted a coup on June 24, 2023, Putin gave a short and fascinating speech on Russian television in which he condemned the "traitors" with the utmost severity: a discourse that was in total contrast to the compromise he seems to have concluded with them a few days later (short-lived given the "accidental" fate of the rebel that followed not long after). In his address to the Russian people that day, a visibly shaken Putin presented himself as the heir of Nicolas II, while clearly distancing himself from his political ancestors, Lenin and the Bolsheviks, who, surfing on World War I, had sacrificed large chunks of Russian territory to take control of power in Petrograd. A large portrait of Nicolas I is supposed to adorn the corridor leading to Putin's office in the Kremlin. An arch-conservative monarch, and the longest tsar in power, only Nicolas I could be the perfect role model for Putin.

Democracy as a danger

To reconstitute the Russian Empire in all its glory sounds like a perfectly legitimate explanation of Putin's revisionist motives. But there is another possible reading of his intention, this one of a more defensive nature. The evolution of Ukraine toward the West in geopolitical, political, economic, and, even more so, cultural terms is perceived by Putin as a great danger for his regime. I remember what my former Ukrainian students at the College of Europe were telling me, calling me from Maidan Square in 2014: "We have been given the choice of being tomorrow a new Poland or a new Belarus. How can we hesitate between the two? We can only dream of moving West, not East." The problem for Putin is that the reasoning of these young Ukrainians could one day extend from Ukraine to Russia and destroy the stability of the current regime in Moscow. Of course, this scenario looks very abstract today. The few Russians who craved freedom and democracy have either left the country or are sitting in jail, if they are not simply already dead like Alexei Navalny. The best and the brightest have left, further compromising the future of Russia in qualitative and quantitative terms, given its falling demographics. It is assumed that more than one million Russians have chosen exile since the beginning of the war in Ukraine, further jeopardizing the future of Russia and its possible access to modernity.

The apathy of the Russian people

The majority of Russians are still behind Putin, even if they can be described more as the "party of apathy" than the "party of conviction." The extreme right-wing nationalists are more like "noisy marginals" than a real force, and even less an alternative source of power for tomorrow's Russia. The only real danger for Putin does not come from them, and certainly not from the pro-democracy camp, but from those who created him more than two decades ago, the FSB (ex KGB) elites. They can turn against Putin if they feel that he endangers their interests and no longer serves the purpose he was chosen for: to restore order and to allow them to get even richer. It would be an exaggeration to depict him as a puppet in their hands, but Putin is probably less powerful than he thinks he is. In the meantime, Russian apathy is exploited with undeniable success by Putin's propaganda machines. Their leaders keep explaining that the special military operations led in Ukraine by Russia's forces were an answer to Western provocations, NATO's aggressive stance in particular, and a precaution vis-à-vis the rebirth of revanchist Nazi forces in Ukraine. Ukrainians thus chose a Jewish president to confuse the world about the true nature of their ideology.

The alibi of NATO enlargement

Of course, the enlargement of NATO to Eastern and Central European countries after the collapse of the Soviet Union, although perfectly justified in political, if not ethical, terms at the close of the Cold War period, could never have been seen as "neutral" by Russia. In 1990, just after the collapse of the Berlin Wall, US Secretary of State James Baker had promised Gorbachev that "the West would not draw a unilateral advantage from the situation." But how could Washington have ever demonstrated to Moscow that NATO's enlargement was purely a political act of inclusion, even a kind of reparation for the West's betrayal and abandonment of the Eastern part of Europe at the end of World War II? And that it was not a preparatory move, albeit a mostly defensive one, in its very nature? Ironically and tragically, Putin's invasion of Ukraine demonstrates a posteriori the strategic necessity of NATO enlargement. What would have happened to the Baltic Republic or even Poland if they had not become part of the Western security military alliance? NATO enlargement certainly contributed to the deterioration of Russian/Western relations, but it is not the cause of the war of aggression launched by Russia in Ukraine. For Putin, it is just an alibi, a pretext. During the NATO summit in Bucharest in 2008, President George W. Bush may have made a mistake in speaking of "an action plan for the adhesion of Ukraine and Georgia" – a move that was supported by the UK, but blocked by France and Germany, these two countries declaring that "Ukraine and Georgia could one day be members of NATO" but certainly not in the near future. The farther away in time, the better.

Why does the South "buy" Putin's rewriting of history?

What is fascinating in the way Putin's rewrites the history of his relations with the West is the fact that his version is "bought" by countries as diverse as China, India, Brazil, and South Africa. In spite of their multiple structural differences, these countries have one thing in common, which allows them to transcend what separates them: they all have a grudge against the West, be it mostly the American or the European West, or both. And with the process of time, resentment, rather than slowly disappearing, seems to become deeper. The scars of the past have become more vivid than ever, the product of anger and despair for some, as in the African continent, the product of growing confidence in themselves for others, as in Asia. Since the beginning of the war in Ukraine, the General Assembly of the United Nations has voted three times on the war in Ukraine, with, on each occasion, more or less identical results: a large majority of countries (around 140) voting to condemn the Russian invasion, but a significant minority (close to 40) choosing to abstain, in spite of the growing revelations of Russia's war crimes, if not crimes against humanity, not to mention the deliberate tactics of nuclear and hunger blackmail practiced by Moscow. It is essential to realize that this minority group represents in demographic terms around 53 percent of the world population. It does not seem to matter to them that Russian imperialism constitutes today the biggest threat to the stability and peace of the world. In their minds, the weight of history, some would say the overweight of the past, continues to prevail.

The anti-Western, anti-NATO narrative of Russia is the ideal one for an imperial power that wants to justify its own interventionist and expansionist predicament. In falsifying reality, Moscow can count on the memories of the close links that existed at the time of the Cold War between the socialist camp and the nonaligned countries. Russia also exploits the dependency on Russian oil and gas of so many countries of the Global South, starting with India, which have been able to get them at discounted prices since the beginning of the war in Ukraine. But although the emotional, anti-Western factor goes well beyond the purely economic rationale, one should not go too far. The Russian/African summit that gathered in Saint Petersburg in the summer of 2023 attracted seventeen African states. There had been forty-three of them in 2019 for the first meeting of that new gathering. Even in the Global South, even in its potentially most favorable part (Africa), the war in Ukraine has contributed to the (relative) isolation of Russia.

To understand the emotional divorce of the world, historical analogies and differences constitute useful tools, even if they may be problematic. The comparison often made between 1938 (the Munich Conference) and today is both legitimate and intriguing. It is difficult to claim that the prospect of NATO enlargement led to the annexation of Crimea in 2014. And it does not make sense to pretend that Hitler's behavior in 1938 was a direct result of the Versailles Peace Treaty and of the excessive severity of the diktat imposed on Germany, with the humiliation of the reparation policies. It was Hitler's perceptions of the weaknesses of Western democracies that ultimately led to World War II. And in the same vein, in the case of Putin, it is neither our arrogance nor our refusal to listen to his demands that led to the war in Ukraine, but Russia's decision to use humiliation as a weapon.

In 1995, the British diplomat Sir Jeremy Greenstock, who went on to become his country's ambassador to the United Nations, coined, in George Kennan fashion, what Western policy toward Russia should be: "Let's engage Russia if we can, let's contain Russia if we must," he elegantly said.

The weaponization of humiliation

Contrary to what Putin wants Russians and members of the Global South to believe, the West did not humiliate Russia; it was Russia that humiliated itself. The country suffered a triple trauma. The first was geopolitical decline following the end of the Soviet Union and the loss of 20 million Russians (or Soviets – a crucial distinction) in the former parts of the empire. During the Cold War period, the Soviet Union was, together with the United States, part of a very select Club of Two: the superpowers. With the collapse of the Soviet Union, this bipolar system was brutally over. The second Russian trauma was of an economic nature. The GDP of the country had fallen by 20 percent in 1991 compared to what it had been in 1989, a level that Russia would not regain until 1997. I have a very vivid memory of that period. I remember in particular a meeting in late 1991 with the then Russian minister for energy. He was very close to a French colleague of mine who was of Russian descent. She had organized a private encounter in her impressive Moscow apartment, built in the purest Stalinist architectural style. As I had recently published a report for a very rich Canadian foundation, the minister for energy was convinced I could help him. In his eyes I was the providential man of the moment. He told me he had no money to pay the employees of his ministry in the coming months. And he was wondering whether the Canadian magnate I had been writing for could advance the money; he would of course be immediately repaid in kind (oil and gas). It was not stated, but it was clear, that were I to accept this go-between role I would receive a generous compensation. I was caught between embarrassment and an irrepressible wish to laugh. I was the least qualified person on earth for the job. I briefly had a vision of the garden of my Normandy home full of gallons of oil and gas. But the story revealed just how desperate for cash Russia was at the time.

The third Russian trauma, probably the most damaging one, was of a psychological nature. It can be described as the combined humiliation of poverty and corruption, in a decomposed political system headed by a political leader, Boris Yeltsin, who was going to prove himself with time to be a growing source of embarrassment. I have a personal recollection of seeing the Master of the Kremlin in the late 1990s, tottering around at the end of an official dinner obviously under the influence of vodka.

The West bears no responsibility for the three traumas mentioned above. On the contrary. The West initially sought – in contrast to what Moscow claims – to slow down the independence of the Baltic Republics and Ukraine. In April 1990, French President François Mitterrand and German Chancellor Helmuth Kohl had jointly written to Vytautas Landsbergis (who was about to become Lithuania's first president since the end of World War II) to beg him to defer the independence of his country. The reasoning behind the Franco-German request sounded as if "one should not replace a distant tyranny by a local despot," a vision that of course had nothing to do with reality. Much more significant even was the speech given to the Ukrainian Parliament in August 1990 by George H. W. Bush, declaring "one must prefer democracy over independence." In early 1991, the wish to exploit Russia's weakness right after the fall of the Soviet Union was more than balanced in Western chancelleries by the fear that a civil war could erupt in the former Soviet Union, on the model of what had just been happening in the former Yugoslavia. Contrary to what Putin pretends today, the West did not wish for, but rather resigned itself to, the de facto division, if not decomposition, of the Soviet Union. In 1991, after the disintegration of the Soviet Empire, Russia was not prevented from playing a role on the world stage. Moscow co-chaired the Arab/Israeli peace process that had opened up in Madrid in 1992 and took part in the contact group presiding over the conflict in Croatia and Bosnia-Herzegovina. Russia was even admitted into the G7, which as a result became the G8 except in financial matters.

In the same manner, the West played no role in the crumbling of the Soviet and post-Soviet economy. Russian economists such as Yegor Gaidar and Anatoly Chubais, advised by Columbia University professor Jeffrey Sachs up until 1995, chose to apply the shock therapy model that had produced elsewhere such spectacular and largely positive results, but that clearly did not work in Russia: a country with much bigger economic flaws and a much more corrupt culture than Poland for example.

The empire of lies

The idea that the West did not speak either to Yeltsin's Russia or, since his coming to power in 2000, to Putin is an absolute lie, a myth forged by Russian propaganda. The West never stopped talking to Putin. The reset policy initiated by President Barack Obama in 2009 was only interrupted in 2014 after the seizure by force of Crimea and the policy of sanctions that followed.

Of course, the Russians, and those sympathetic to their cause, can evoke the precedents of Western military interventionism from Kosovo to Afghanistan, from Iraq to Libya. And it is fair to say that, seen from Moscow, the case of Kosovo is troubling. In this case, were not boundary changes obtained by force? And NATO's campaign against Slobodan Milošević's Serbia started without the assent of the UN Security Council, thus constituting a first serious turning point in the relations between Russia and the West. I have a vivid memory of this period. I was in a small campus close to Moscow at that time, teaching the subject of democracy to a group of members of the Duma (the Russian Parliament) within the framework of a school I had contributed to create: the Moscow School for Political Studies. The very open and liberal members of this group reacted very negatively to my defense – on human rights grounds – of Western action in the Balkans. I remember quoting the terms of a high-level US diplomat who, in his office in Washington on the eve of NATO's intervention, was telling me: "We in America cannot remain passive, when we see civilians forced into trains in Europe. We were much too slow to react during World War II, we are not going to repeat the same mistakes." If only Milošević had heard these words and taken them seriously. My Russian students were not impressed. They felt, as fellow Slavs, humiliated by Western attitudes, deceived by NATO.

In the hands of Putin, as in those of many leaders of the South, humiliation, coupled with anger, has been weaponized, in a systematic and not always sophisticated, yet very efficient, manner. Like children, they tend to repeat the same accusation: "It's not fair." So many things may be unfair. The feeling of injustice may signify: "We were just emerging from the period of COVID. We thought the worse was behind us and suddenly we have to ask ourselves if it is not ahead of us. Could the war among nations succeed the war against COVID?"

But we were all equals in the face of the pandemic. It affected the rich as well as the poor, the powerful as much as the powerless. Contrary to what one feared, the economically and socially weakest continents were not the worst affected by the pandemic. This could have been because they are demographically the youngest or because the lack of hygiene contributed to reinforcing the immune systems of populations. The war in Ukraine may also be perceived as a sort of equalizer, with the return of war on a continent that had been spared from it for nearly eighty years, thanks to Franco-German reconciliation and the American security guarantee. The return of war in Europe will not constitute a source of comfort for the populations of Myanmar or Sudan confronted with the dark realities of civil war. But at a time when the rich become even richer, and the poor comparatively poorer, the European war, at least in pure emotional terms, brings us back to a more "balanced world." We are not equals in our relationship with climate change or war – some continents are more affected than others – but we are all touched in one way or another.

What should the West's answer be?

Our answer has to be firm and clear. The empire of lies uses fear to destabilize us. Putin is convinced that time plays in his favor. His reasoning goes as follows. The motivation of the Russian army may be inferior to that of the Ukrainians, but it is nevertheless superior to that of the Western world. Between sheer fatigue and the fear of escalation into World War III, Putin firmly believes that a complacent and selfish West will ultimately cave in and accept a compromise, whatever its cost for the Ukrainians. His implicit message is as follows: "You are not going to risk your hedonistic, comfortable lifestyle for the sake of Ukraine, a country that has never really existed, and that is at least as fundamentally corrupt as Russia."

In this battle of political will, we simply have to prove Putin wrong.

On top of the indecisiveness and channel-switching temperament of the West, Putin is convinced that he has a potentially decisive weapon: the American electorate who has returned Trump to power. This simply means that the frailty of the United States has to be compensated for by the new strength and determination of the Europeans. The war is taking place on the European Continent. Ukraine is a European nation, it is part of us, it is us. To betray Ukraine would be to betray ourselves. It would send the worst of messages to Putin's Russia: "We prefer to be 'protected' by you than to resist you at all costs, including the risk of escalation into a global war." This argument, Putin is convinced of it, will grow with time. It is already shared by the extreme right and the extreme left of the Western political spectrum on both sides of the Atlantic, not to mention some Gaullist elements of the more classical right in France for example. Absolute pacifist feelings, when reinforced by lingering anti-American calculus and emotions, become a powerful weapon in the arms of Moscow.

"Don't be afraid"

The only way to fight fear and lies is through information and knowledge. If you can't have freedom from danger, you can have freedom from fear. "Don't be afraid" was the key message of Pope John Paul II, a message that played a decisive role in the fate of Eastern Europe, in particular his homeland Poland, and more globally in the collapse of the Berlin Wall and the disintegration of the Soviet Union. "Don't be afraid" is the only way to confront Putin today. To ignore the danger he represents for Europe and the world is an illusion, a form of escapism. But to succumb to fear is precisely what Putin wants.

"Absolute security for one actor, means absolute insecurity for all others," remarked the French philosopher Raymond Aron in his magnus opus *Peace and War*. By invading Ukraine, Russia demonstrated at the same time how weak it deemed the West to be, but also how deeply insecure it feels. I remember a Russian friend telling me in the early 2010s that the election of Barack Obama and the acceptance of same-sex marriage were seen in the Kremlin as outright confirmation of America's decline. This infamous comment was just proof of the racism and homophobia that dominated (and still dominates) in the mind of Russia's top leadership. But as is most often the case, this downgrading of the "other," for the color of their skin, sexual preferences, etc., hides a deep sense of insecurity in identity terms. The more diverse and complex the world becomes, the more Russia feels it is losing control of its identity. Russians can compare the demographic and economic strength of countries such as India (one human out of six is Indian) or China with its own weaknesses. There is a dimension of self-fulfilling prophecy in Putin's behavior. Confronted with the decline of Russia's economy and demography, the inevitable (if hidden) erosion of his popularity after more than two decades in power, Putin uses war the way Napoleon III did with the Franco-Prussian war in 1870/71 – with the catastrophic results that followed for his regime. One can refer too to the calculus of the Russian and Austro-Hungarian Empires on the eve of World War I. A "good little war" would reinforce the two imperial powers in decline. As a result, they both disappeared. But one comparison came spontaneously to my mind on the early morning of February 24, 2022: Putin as a modern-day Napoleon I. Putin's invasion of Ukraine would, I felt, constitute for him the equivalent of what the invasion of Russia meant for Napoleon in 1812: the beginning of the end. I am still convinced that this scenario remains, in one way or the other, the most likely one, even though it is far from obvious – as long, of course, as Ukraine and her allies remain united in their respective resilience. Putin has defined the struggle against the West in terms of civilization. Decadent and obsolete democracies on the one hand; virile, modern, and efficient autocracies on the other. The Western world must accept that challenge. Russia is not China. Dependence on Russia has been drastically reduced, thanks to Putin, who has pushed "us," in particular in Europe, in the right, "green" ecological direction by forcing us to break our dependence on Russian oil. Having drastically (though not sufficiently) reduced the dimension of greed thanks to a combination of sanctions including embargos, we are left with the argument of fear. Putin can brandish his nuclear arsenal, but can he really use it? He has been constantly playing to the utmost the Chinese card. But there are intrinsic limits to that choice. Xi Jinping may accept being associated with a modern version of Ivan the Terrible, but not with a reincarnation of Hitler. And that is how Putin would be viewed if nuclear weapons, even at the pure tactical level, were to be used. The spectacular movie *Oppenheimer*, realized by the British director Christopher Nolan, which came out in the summer of 2023, a biopic about the life of one of the fathers of the atomic bomb and the director of the Manhattan Project, constitutes from that standpoint a wake-up call as to the unique nature of the nuclear weapon. It remains to be seen whether such a movie can contribute to further isolate Putin's blackmail practices, or, on the contrary, reinforce the pacifist argument used by all those who want a compromise at the expense of Ukraine, and this as soon as possible.

To conclude

The war in Ukraine can be seen and understood as an archeological site full of layers of analogies. The contrast between the paucity of territorial gains and the number of casualties on both sides evokes the trench war of World War I in Europe. The ideological and Manichean nature of the conflict as seen by the West and the East reminds us of World War II. It is not right versus left, but right versus wrong. The comparison between Putin and Hitler comes to mind, in an almost irresistible way. And as far as the scenario for the future is concerned, the comparison with the Korean war and the armistice that has prevailed since 1953 seems to be one of the most plausible, if no side can win decisively. Ukraine would be added to the long list of unresolved problematic nations from Cyprus to Israel/ Palestine and so many others.

The reference to the 1938 Munich Conference is often mentioned too, as an indication of the possible betrayal of Ukraine by its Western allies. A betrayal that would, in this case, be the result of the fear of escalation of a war that has already started, and not to prevent (without any success) the coming of war, as in 1938.

In a BBC "Reith Lecture" given in early 2023, Fiona Hill, the British-American foreign affairs expert and Russia specialist, made an interesting comparison. For her, the Russian invasion of Ukraine was as outrageous as would have been an attempt by the UK to reconquer by force the Republic of Ireland, thirty years after having granted its independence.

But at the end of the day, the war in Ukraine is above all a conflict of emotions. Imperial emotions on the Russian side, national emotions on the Ukrainian side. Who will give in first? The ultimate result may be decided on the battlefield, but not necessarily so. Here again, emotions will play a key role. One can assume the Ukrainians will not flinch. Each new Russian crime reinforces their determination. They have already suffered so much. Resigning themselves to a return to normality with the accepted loss of territories conquered by Russians is simply unacceptable, even if some kind of deal could be reached in the end. Ukrainians could (temporarily?), in exchange for full entrance into NATO and the EU, accept having 17–20 percent of their territory – Crimea and the zones occupied by Moscow before 2022 – under the control of the Russians. Too big a sacrifice? It would simply imply a redefinition of the meaning of victory. For not to lose the war means victory for Ukraine, whereas not to clearly win means defeat for Russia. What is to be prevented is a clear-cut Russian victory that would encourage Moscow's appetite for other adventures in Europe. Such a scenario would imply that Ukrainians are able to transcend their emotions and that Russians have no other choice and have to realize they have no ways of winning the war on their own terms.

The emotions of the Russians, on the one hand, and of their pro-Russian Ukrainian allies, on the other, are even less predictable. On the side of Kiev's allies, will fatigue in face of the war, and fear of its escalation, progressively replace the power of indignation, on the one hand, and the fear of an expansionist Russia, on the other? It will largely depend on what happens on the battlefield. No one likes to support for long a losing side.

On the Russian side, Putin has managed at the same time to mobilize the Russians against the so-called war of aggression led by the West, but without asking too much from them, as if he knew intuitively that a majority of Russians in their general apathy were perhaps ready to make some sacrifices for their motherland, but not the supreme one, i.e. the sacrifice of their lives for the return of Ukraine under Russian influence, if not total control. In the majority of the major Russian cities, from Moscow to Saint Petersburg for example, life is as normal as possible. Apart from the Ukrainian drones that from time to time reach Russian territory, it would be impossible to guess that a war is going on. This may constitute one of Putin's greatest challenges. Without some form of escalation, including a greater mobilization of the Russian people, the Master of the Kremlin will fail to achieve his military and political goal of controlling Ukraine. But in order to reach this goal, he runs the risk of further isolating himself from the Russian people. In other words, in order to consolidate his power at home and his image abroad, he may be losing control of his destiny. One does not see any obvious successor to Putin, but nature abhors a vacuum.

2

The Emergence of the Global South

A surreal interview

It was more than four decades ago, in 1984. I had only just landed in Seoul after a short flight from Tokyo and was entering my hotel room when the phone rang. It was Korean television. They wanted to interview me on the future of North/South relations. I was half surprised. I was not an economist, but a French specialist of international relations (the expression geopolitics was not used at that time), coming from a country where the former president, Valéry Giscard d'Estaing, had launched the idea of a new and bold initiative for the creation of a North/South world economic order. The questions asked by the Korean TV crew were very general and centered on one theme: was I optimistic about the future of that relationship? The more prudent and banal my answers were, the more satisfied my interlocutors seemed: "In the long run one should be optimistic, but in the short run, one should not expect too much," was the gist of my thinking.

It was only a few hours later, when dining with the French ambassador at his residence in Seoul, that I realized my confusion. The North/South future the interview was focusing on did not concern the future of the world economic order, but the future of relations between South and North Korea. For more than ten minutes on primetime Korean television, I had given a totally surreal interview. Were the journalists aware of my confusion and too polite to interrupt me, or were my prudent and general warnings in line with what they expected a foreigner to say? Less than a decade later, the reunification of West and East Germany had reinforced the position of those in the South who thought that, given its enormous economic cost for "Wessies" (West Germans), it was urgent to wait, or at least not to hurry the process, if only for financial and budgetary reasons.

This story still haunts me, as a form of dual warning. First, one should never grant interviews when one is not certain what the topic is going to be about. And second and more seriously, the very term "North/South relations" covers many (at times mutually exclusive) interpretations.

What is the Global South today?

The Global South today is both a geopolitical and an economic reality – something that was not the case during the Cold War years. It brings together extremely diverse countries that one would hardly place in the same group were it not for one major shared trait: they all define themselves with respect to the West, if not actually against it. In emotional terms, their starting point is a mixture of hope for what they aspire to become one day, combined with a deep frustration, even anger, at the way, the West has treated them in the past and continues to do (at least in their eyes) in the present. Such frustration spans the entire chronological period starting with the colonial/imperial years, moving on to the mismanaged decolonization process, before shaping the geopolitical issues that have emerged since the end of the Cold War.

The West has mismanaged the world

In a powerful essay published in *Foreign Affairs* in May/June 2023, "The World beyond Ukraine: The survival of the West and the demands of the rest," David Miliband, former UK Secretary of State for Foreign and Commonwealth Affairs, explains how the unified and concerted action of the West in response to the war in Ukraine shocked the countries of the Global South. It contrasted vividly with the numerous occasions when the West violated its own rules (as in Iraq in 2003) or failed to apply them (as in Syria in 2013, when Obama did not react to the crossing of a red line – the use by the Assad regime of chemical weapons against its own population). For the Global South, doing the right thing in Ukraine was perceived as an alibi for doing very little, if anything, in the rest of the world. Whatever the nature of their regimes, whether democracies such as Brazil, India, Indonesia, and South Africa, or not (the majority of countries in the Global South), what prevailed was a feeling that the West had double standards. I would personally use the expression of selective emotions. This anger of the Global South is compounded by a deep sense of frustration at stalled reform efforts in the international system. Prominent Indian diplomat Shivshankar Menon claims: "Alienated and resentful, many developing countries see the war in Ukraine and the West's rivalry with China as distracting from urgent issues such as debt, climate change, and the effects of the pandemic." Without wanting to take issue with Menon, one can still reply that the primary responsibility for this gigantic distraction comes from Russia's territorial appetite and China's historical hurry in wanting to have its regional, if not world, supremacy to be recognized *now*.

At the same time, to be fair, one has to acknowledge the weakness of the American position after Donald Trump's first presidency. How can the United States claim to defend global norms after demonstrating for four years such utter contempt for global rules in areas as diverse as climate change, human rights, and nuclear nonproliferation? How can one preach to the world principles one no longer applies either domestically or internationally?

Miliband argues: "The West has failed, since the financial crisis of 2008, to show that it is willing or able to drive forward a more equal and sustainable global economic bargain or to develop the political institutions appropriate to manage a multipolar world." In 2022, more than 100 million people fled for their lives from war or disaster. According to the UN, more than 350 million people needed humanitarian aid, compared to 81 million in 2013. More than 600 million Africans (nearly one out of four) have no access to electricity. The risks of the West failing to respect its priorities by not funding its programs can only deepen the trust deficit, while strengthening ideological challenges to Western liberal, democratic principles. The climate crisis is of course the global risk that looms largest and constitutes the greatest test of Western sincerity in terms of solidarity with the rest of the world.

The underrepresentation of the Global South

Beyond the criticisms of the dual standards of the West, there is in the Global South frustration at being underrepresented in the world's international institutions. These institutions, foremost among them the UN, were created when decolonization had not even begun. In eight decades of their existence, none has been reformed. The frustrations of the Global South are thus more than understandable. The Global South needs (and deserves) a greater say in the international arena, which ultimately means a permanent seat (indeed, more than one) at the "real" table, i.e. the UN Security Council. Throughout the years, and in different institutions, I have had many conversations with top French diplomats on this topic, and their argument always remained the same. They were explaining to me with candor, why they were so openly favorable to an enlargement in the composition of the Security Council. Their main argument was, bluntly put, as follows: "I am for it, because it cannot happen. It is simply impossible to achieve." Or, "France may not deserve her seat, in today's conditions, but why should she give it up? It would be senseless to abandon one of the few comparative advantages (together with her nuclear military status), France has over Germany."

I encountered once, and once only, a sincere openness on the subject. Jean François-Poncet, who was France's foreign minister under the presidency of Valéry Giscard d'Estaing (1974–81), toyed with the idea that France and the UK should give up their permanent seats at the UN Security Council to create a joint seat for the EU. In his mind, this enlightened generosity would resolve the question of a German seat (not to speak of Italy) and would promote Europe's identity on the world stage. It was of course nothing more than an indulgent utopia. Neither London nor Paris was willing to abandon such a key element of their status and influence.

Can the Global South save the UN?

Misrepresentation and inequality have persisted up till now. The five permanent members of the Security Council – China, France, Russia, the United Kingdom, and the United States – have kept the right to veto any resolution, thereby side-lining the other ten non-permanent members, many of which are low- to middle-income countries. This veto-right has led to paralysis and de facto impunity for countries that have committed mass atrocities. In 2022, more than 100 countries signed a resolution presented by France and Mexico that called for the permanent members of the Security Council to agree to refrain from using their veto rights in cases of mass atrocity. Such a proposal definitely goes in the right direction, but it is clearly not sufficient. The UN is faced with an inner contradiction. The less representative the composition of the Security Council, the less legitimate the entire organization becomes. But the veto-right, given in 1945 at the time of its creation to its five permanent members, makes any change in its composition simply impossible unless a major disaster (a nuclear war, for example) were to open the selfish eyes of the Club of Five. The Portuguese António Guterres is one of the best UN secretary-generals of its history, but his qualities are largely wasted, given the limited margin of maneuver at his disposal. In the late 1990s I was asked by Secretary-General Kofi Annan to join a very informal group of mostly public opinion-makers, who met with him in the former Rockefeller mansion, in the vicinity of New York. It was at the end of the Balkan wars. I still remember an exchange with him. I remember telling him that I thought it was essential for the UN to take the clearest of positions in the Balkans, especially after the resounding failure of the organization to make a difference in Rwanda (a time when Kofi Annan himself was the UN defense minister; the real title was deputy secretary-general). I could thus see at first hand the dilemmas of an organization that should have been more properly termed "the Disunited States of the World." Aware of his incapacity to beef up the hard power of the UN – in spite of a brief honeymoon period with the United States and its permanent representative Richard Holbrooke during Bill Clinton's second term in office – Kofi Annan chose to concentrate on the reinforcement of the soft power of the secretary-general. As it stands today, the UN is more the incarnation of what goes wrong in the world than the beginning of a solution to its problems. And it will remain so, at least as long as no country of the Global South is represented in its Security Council, foremost among them India. At the same time, it is clear, the United Nations does not improve its image when it entrusts the presidency of the Social Forum of its Human Rights Commission to a country like Iran, which uses systematically violent repression against its own society, women in particular.

A period of transition between two worlds

It is essential to understand that we live in a period of transition between two worlds. The old order no longer works, but is not dead, and the new one is still in limbo. Everything is possible, all scenarios are open. The emergence of a Global South is one key component of this entrance into a new era.

But the definition of the Global South itself is very confusing, if not paradoxical. Apart from an element of negative identity toward the West, the countries that constitute the Global South come from continents whose results, weight, and perception of themselves differ greatly. Not all Asian countries are successful (far from it), but the large majorities of the success stories come from Asia. From that standpoint, Asia is still the continent of hope. Africa and Latin America, on the other hand, the two continents that, in *The Geopolitics of Emotion* I bundled together as "hard cases," for no single emotion clearly prevailed over others, have evolved, unfortunately, more negatively than positively. There is undeniably more despair and anger in Africa and Latin America than was the case in 2009. The case of the Middle East is more ambivalent. Saudi Arabia has reacted to America's (its former grand protector) loss of control in the region by, to plagiarize Frank Sinatra, "doing it her way." Under the muscular leadership of MBS, the kingdom has engaged on a path to modernity, whose main religion is sacred selfishness. The kingdom navigates between competing great powers in a spectacular illustration of pure realpolitik. Riyad has accepted the mediation of Beijing to restart diplomatic relations with Tehran, and, to add insult to injury for Washington, did not hesitate to raise significantly the price of its oil, despite America's gentle pressures. And the Saudis, although not yet ready to formalize their diplomatic relations with Israel, essentially deal with the Hebrew state, as if the Palestinian problem did not exist – a position that is no longer tenable after October 7, 2023. It has been said that the ultimate goal of Hamas (and beyond, of its protector Iran) was to render impossible any form of rapprochement between Riyad and Jerusalem.

Israel in between two worlds

As for Israel itself, it is undeniably part of the West, but in political and social terms it embodies most of what has gone wrong with the West. In fact, in its current political and societal polarization, Israel can be perceived as the avant-garde in terms of what is endangering the Western democratic model. With the coming to power in 2022 of the most right-wing coalition in the history of the country since its creation, the Hebrew state is now faced with a deeply divided citizenry on the very institutional fundamentals of the country. Netanyahu in Israel, Trump in America, and, for that matter, Putin in Russia are not just actors responsible for the respective evolutions of their countries, but rather symptoms of each country's deeply negative developments. For reasons we will analyze in the following chapters, the causes of the problems facing Israel, the United States, and Russia precede the coming to power of their respective leaders. In the specific case of Israel, are we confronted with the dark side of the West's identity crisis, or should we say instead – looking at the deepening religious fanaticism of a growing part of the population – of the beginning of the Middle Easternization of the country? In a powerful book published in 2013, *Israel Has Moved*, the French/American historian of Italian descent, Diana Pinto, described the identity crisis facing the Hebrew state. Israelis initially came from Europe, but they maintained a distance with the continent that had destroyed two-thirds of the Jews; they then started to distance themselves from the United States and were tempted to move toward Asia economically. Could we say that, in its relations with Washington, the Hebrew state is simply "hedging its bets," with respect to a country that does not know where it is going, that has of late become very critical of the Jewish state's right-wing orientations, and that is now confronted at home with a significant surge in antisemitism, which has increased significantly since the beginning of the Gaza war?

From the Third World to the Global South

In the 1960s, the concept of the South was, above all, of an economic nature. It referred to the poor underdeveloped parts of the world, in opposition to the rich North. The expression "Third World," which started to be coined around that time, had a dual advantage. It allowed us to bypass the expression "underdevelopment," or the more optimistic "developing countries" formula. The Third World could be seen politically as the perfect description of the group of the nonaligned countries, those that refused to choose between the Western and communist blocs, between two sorts of imperialism, both the product of Western culture, be it capitalist or socialist. Of course, the Soviet Union, in its willingness to destabilize the West, supported all the liberation movements against its former colonial powers. In 1948, Moscow even recognized Israel before the United States with the clear objective of weakening the British Empire.

But the Global South of today is much more the direct product of the nonaligned movement of yesterday than the heir of the Third World. And yet there are major differences between the two. At the time of the Bandung (a city on the island of

Java in Indonesia) Conference in 1955, which launched the nonaligned movement, decolonization was still an ongoing process. And the mostly Asian/African conference attracted countries that were promoting peaceful coexistence, economic development, and an end to all form of racial discrimination. Sukarno in Indonesia and Nehru in India both played a major role. Zhou Enlai, who was representing China, was more than just a forerunner of the future, for China's intervention in the Indochina war had just proved decisive and had forced France to recognize her defeat.

But the economic weight of Asia and Africa remained modest at that time and there was no indisputable leader of the movement. In fact, the nonaligned movement reached crisis point quite rapidly, as early as the late 1960s, the disappearance of the Egyptian leader Gamel Abdel Nasser in 1970 confirming that evolution. They had slowly moved closer to the Soviet Union, in large part as a result of the Vietnam War. Their nonalignment was tilting more and more toward the East.

From the nonaligned movement to the Global South

The transformation of the nonaligned movement into the Global South is the consequence of major changes. Geopolitically, the Cold War had ended. Economically, the rise of Asia has been so spectacular that one can say that the rich were becoming as common in the South as in the North. One proof of this has been the rising number of billionaires coming from China and India.

But the most important factor in this change lies elsewhere. Contrary to the nonaligned movement of the past, the Global South of today has an emerging and very clear potential leader: India. This is a country whose declared ambition is to elevate the Global South and which sees its primary mission as representing the voices of the South in the international arena. Yet one should not take this vision of Prime Minister Modi at face value, especially given the worrisome rise of Indian religious nationalism. Nevertheless, the comparison between India's and China's visions of themselves is very revealing. For the case of China can be confusing. The Middle-Empire could claim to be the indisputable leader of the Global South. But it does not. For reasons we will develop in the following chapter, China is the leader of the revisionist and aggressive Global East, much more than that of the Global South. It aims to be number one in the world, and not only in Asia. And it wants to be recognized as such by the entire planet, as soon as possible. China is not "in between," a role that can only seem demeaning. It sees itself as a number one in the making, at one extreme of the ideological spectrum. There is no compromise in its position, just strong certitudes and extremely well-defined ambitions and goals.

India: the potential rise of a new giant

In early 2012, I was the guest of a special visitor's program organized by the Indian foreign ministry. The culminating point of my trip was a nearly two-hour-long bilateral meeting with Prime Minister Singh's then national security advisor Shivshankar Menon, a man sometimes described as India's Henry Kissinger. Menon had read my book, *The Geopolitics of Emotion*, and wanted to discuss it, in particular the passages on Indian emotions. I still remember vividly his concluding remarks at the end of our conversation. I will summarize them in a few sentences. "The world expects a lot from India, in fact too much. If you want to understand where we stand today, you have to compare India to what America was in the immediate aftermath of World War I. Like Americans in the early twentieth century, we are not ready and prepared for the role the world wants us to play. Unlike Chinese or Russians, we are not naturally at ease with power. We have no recent Imperial tradition of our own. We were ruled by the British for more than two centuries and before them by a Moghul Moslem Empire that was largely foreign to our essence. And we have a deep pacifist tradition, whose strongest incarnation was of course Gandhi. We have been independent for a little more than sixty years [our conversation took place in 2012]. We are not in a hurry to play geopolitics in the big league alongside the United States or China. It's not in our blood, it is not in our genes."

This modesty, sincere or partly feigned, this deliberate restraint on the part of India, belongs to another world. In less than a decade, moving from Singh to Modi, India's ambition has grown exponentially. The international and regional contexts have also drastically changed, along with India's economic reality and leadership. Do Indians today have the choice to be restrained in their approach to the world? With its population and economy forecast to continue to grow rapidly over the coming decades, India is increasingly seen as the ideal and now credible counterweight to China, strategically but also in the future economically. Entrepreneurship in the country is abundant and infrastructure is improving. If we assume that India's GDP per head will continue to grow at 5 percent a year, while that of the US grows at 1.4 percent, more or less what it has done in the last three decades, India will not only be a great power, but its economy will be of a similar size to that of the US by 2050.

As for leadership, for better or (and) for worse, Narendra Modi incarnates India's and to a large extent too, Asia's incredibly rapid coming of age.

In truth, the change has been spectacular. At the end of World War II, India and Asia were still largely colonized; India was poor, backward, and weak. Today, Asia is at the center of world politics. China and India have eliminated more poverty in a shorter amount of time than any other nation in history: a source of legitimate national and regional pride.

A giant threatened by itself

But there is a catch. Under Prime Minister Modi, Indian nationalism has taken on a dangerously emotional religious connotation. A nation so proud of its open, "argumentative" culture, to quote Nobel prizewinner Amartya Sen, is aiming to exclude more than 200 million Muslim citizens from its vision for the future. How can India's global ambition be attained without the full inclusion, support, and collaboration of all its citizens? How can India be so proud of her status as the largest democracy in the world if not all of its citizens are treated equally? From that standpoint, it is tempting to make a comparison between India and Israel, whatever the huge and obvious differences between two countries that reached independence at the same time. A religious brand of nationalism, the flirtation with illiberal democracy of their two respective leaders: Modi and Netanyahu. India has not solved its problem with its Muslim minority, and Israel has deliberately ignored its Israeli Arab citizens, and the Palestinians in general – even if, in both cases, one should refrain from giving simplistic lessons from the outside.

According to the American think-tank Freedom House, India is, on the democratic front, at the same level as Hungary, the country whose leader, Victor Orbán, coined the expression "illiberal democracy." According to Freedom House, political rights, electoral politics in particular, are healthier in India than in Hungary, but civil rights are weaker. At the same time, India's ratings on democracy are far higher than those of Pakistan, Bangladesh, or even Turkey. Yet, according to the World Bank indicators, as quoted by Martin Wolf in his column in the *Financial Times* ("Modi's India is moving in an illiberal direction," July 25, 2023), as India has become less liberal, its government has become more effective. Political stability and the absence of violence, control of corruption, and regulatory quality have all improved since the coming of

Narendra Modi to power in 2014. But voice and accountability, and even more so the rule of law in general, have worsened. In short, is there an inevitable balance between repression and effectiveness? Does one need more of the first to have more of the second?

The key question is elsewhere and is the direct result of identity politics. For today's Hindu nationalists, "a true Indian must be Hindu." To reject that new reality is anti-national, and therefore to be a traitor. What we are increasingly confronted with in India is simply the dictatorship of the majority, if not the despotic temptation of one very charismatic man. Without freedom of opinion and opposition, competitive democracy cannot function. Why should a predominantly Hindu society not tolerate minority faiths, minority rights? It is all the more depressing that this evolution contradicts the fundamentals of a culture that is inherently tolerant. According to a 2021 study of religious attitudes conducted by the Pew Foundation, 85 percent of Hindus, who represent 80 percent of the population, believe "respecting all religions is very important to be truly Indian." The ambition to create a modern, prosperous, and strong India is in conflict with the resort to identity politics in the most intolerant and backward manner.

Yet the negative direction taken by identity politics should not obscure the growing self-confidence of a country that has just become number one in the world in terms of demography. The responsibility to feed and educate one-sixth of the world population could be seen economically and socially as a discouraging challenge. But in India, it is perceived above all as a source of irresistible energy and success. For the country is collectively moved by a sense of revenge toward its recent history (the Raj period) and the deep conviction that India's time has come because the country has reached maturity precisely at the very moment its most direct rivals, China and the United States, are reaching their limits and are faced with deep inner contradictions. This spirit of revenge against humiliation is, in the Indian case too, a strong weapon. This can be seen in two popular movies that were great successes both in India and internationally. The first one is *Lagaan*, an exciting tale about a village that, at the very beginning of the twentieth century, defeats the arrogant British colonial power in a game of cricket, thanks to the help of a British teacher who came to the defense of their apparently lost cause. The peasants refused to pay newly increased taxes. And, as a provocation of sorts, the local British officer suggested to the villagers that if they prevailed at cricket, they would pay no taxes at all. But if they were defeated – by far the most likely outcome – the level of taxes paid by the villagers would be doubled.

The second movie, much more recent, *RRR*, received the Oscar (an absolute first for an Indian movie in that competition) for the best lyrics. Taking place around the 1920s, the action, as in *Lagaan*, ridicules the British and celebrates the charm and virility of Indian versus British males, through spectacular dancing and singing. *RRR* was a triumph throughout Asia, as if the entire Indo/Asian continent recognized itself in this Indian victory over the West.

These popular movies demonstrate a deeper reality that emerges in the dance scenes of *RRR* with their unique youthful energy that seems to combine Indian tradition and bebop. India's soft power is not only benefiting from the youthful energy of its actors and dancers, but also – some would say more seriously – from the respective decline of Chinese and American soft power, which can be seen in two opposite realities. China seems too strong for the good of its neighbors, while America is increasingly perceived as too weak for the safety of its allies, because of its internal divisions. (It would be dangerously premature though to bury the attractiveness and creativity of American culture. The worldwide triumph of the movie *Barbie* is a clear indicator of the resilience of America's popular culture.)

In between China and the United States, India looks like a perfect compromise. The country is not threatening any one, unlike China (or Russia), and it seems to have a bright future, and this not only because of the youthful energies of its powerful demographics. And India has no imperial past, unlike America, Europe, or even (though they claim not to have one) China. India has managed to navigate shrewdly through the new complexities of international realities. It is at the same time close to the United States, a counterbalance to China, and close to Russia for a mixture of energy and military reasons. But it is also very close to Israel, and not only in order to please the United States. The two countries are united by the existence of a common threat: Islamic fundamentalism.

The balancing force in Asia

Ideally, though they do not yet formulate it with such clarity, Indians are aiming at becoming the balancing force in Asia, between China and the United States, in the way their former imperial power, Great Britain, had been for Europe and the world during most of the nineteenth century. What a symbolic revenge such a scenario would be. There is almost an emotional parallel between France's ambition of strategic autonomy for Europe and Modi's international ambition. Could India be the privileged partner for a Europe that has the ambition to become a power in its own right? It is far from certain that Europe will attain this goal, but it is crystal clear that India has, more successfully than Europe, realized that it must confront China, and realizes it may have to do so without the United States. India, like Macron's Europe, dreams of strategic autonomy and wants to stay out of the logic of blocs. Delhi works with a coalition of powers, wherever India's interests coincide with those of others. But this legitimate goal must be pursued with prudence and not in a flashy manner. India should not repeat the mistakes of China and fall prey to the temptation to become the equivalent of Germany in the years that preceded World War I – a Germany that shifted from the prudent policy of Bismarck to the aggressive one of Wilhelm II. As Shavshankar Menon writes in the conclusion of his book *India and Asian Geopolitics*: "This is not a time for drama, showy events and the pursuit of status. India's powers and capabilities have yet to peak, and no other power shares its interests. Influence like power is a means to an end."

But how does one exercise self-containment when the energy that fuels one's ambition comes in large part from one's sense of humiliation and a desire for revenge? How can one refrain from saying "My time has come," when reality is more complex and more subtle, when the right formula should be "My time may be coming, if I do all the right things, even more so internally, than externally"? Germany and Japan tried and failed in the last century to box above their weight, with terrible consequences for them and the world.

Yet it is my deep belief that India is not a "country with a future, and that will remain so for ever," as people say when they speak in a derogatory manner of Brazil. A country that will fail to make it. India is different from Brazil, first of all because it is situated in the right geographical context: Asia and not Latin America.

India benefits also of the ambiguity of Chinese identity. The land of Gandhi is clearly an integral part of the Global South, in fact its natural leader; whereas China may be perceived more easily as the obvious leader of the Global East, a small but significant group of "aggressive" countries that regroups China, Russia, North Korea, and probably Iran, and whose revisionist ambition is to succeed the West, not only in terms of power, but also as a political model. Paradoxically, the greatest obstacle to the realization of India's dream of power and influence may be Modi himself. How can a country/continent so proud to present itself as "the mother of democracies" be led by a man flirting with "enlightened despotism"?

The Global South beyond India

The other key actors of the Global South are Brazil, Indonesia, Nigeria, South Africa, Turkey, and a newcomer already mentioned, which is using its immense wealth and the tenacious determination of its new leader to play above its station: Saudi Arabia.

The particular case of Turkey

A key member of NATO, and as such part of the West, and still a candidate for EU membership – even if it has no illusions about ever integrating into a "Christian Club" – Erdoğan's Turkey perceives itself both as the legitimate inheritor of the Ottoman Empire from the Middle East to Central Asia, and as a key Muslim (mostly Sunni) country. On these two fronts, Turkey is the direct rival of an Iran that does not forget in spite of its ultra-religious Muslim nationalism (mostly Shi'ite) that it is the proud heir of the Persian Empire.

Asian in its economic ambitions, Western in its institutional engagements, much more so than in its deep emotions, Turkey is also, and maybe above all, Middle Eastern. The two great non-Arab powers, Turkey and Iran, seem to pursue the same objective: to exist as an opposing force – indirectly in the case of Turkey, much more brutally in the case of Iran – not only against the West, but against all those who in the Arab world seem to be tempted to play the game of the West by getting closer to Israel. There is another factor unifying Turkey and Iran, despite the very significant differences between them: illiberal democracy characterizes the former, religious despotism describes the latter. In their foreign engagements, both countries seem to be searching for some kind of counterweight to the growing unpopularity of their regimes, much deeper of course in the case of Iran. Erdoğan was re-elected in the presidential elections of 2023. But in the 2024 municipal elections, his candidates were defeated, if not humiliated, by moderate forces that this time had found weighty and credible candidates.

Africa: the forgotten continent

In 1943, W. E. B. Du Bois, a leading American scholar and civil rights activist with communist sympathies, asked himself how capitalism and race relations were influencing World War II. He went as far as arguing that the ongoing conflict was a competition for colonies. "It was a white's man war," he wrote. It is important to keep this in mind when we consider African attitudes to the war in Ukraine. The parallel between the past and the present is clear. But there is another dimension of temporal continuity that is even more preoccupying. For many people in Africa think (rightly?) that China, the United States, Russia, and Europe still view their continent as an arena for competition, rather than as a place of importance in its own right. In 1943, allied powers were already drawing plans for the political and economic reconstruction of the world. But in their vision, there was no mention of Africa, at most a vague reference. Isn't the West confronted with an ongoing dual tragic continuity? Today, as in the past, Africa is still betrayed by others, but it is also betrayed by its own elites. In the early 2000s, in spite of all its difficulties, Africa could be seen as the continent of hope, with its youthful demographic profile and unique natural resources. Is this still the case today? And if not, what has happened? The vision of thousands of Africans risking their lives to find a future in Europe must play a major role in our reasoning. Since 2018, more than 100,000 migrants, mostly Africans, have crossed the Channel to find a new life in Great Britain, for example. Rationally, we should have transcended a purely (and largely hypocritical given the results) humanitarian discourse on Africa. For the African continent is a huge economic and geopolitical challenge. And Europe, now an aging continent, where birth rates are falling (even in France, where until recently the opposite was the case), badly needs the young energy coming from Africa and the Middle East. But emotionally we are not prepared to receive them, or to vet candidates for emigration inside their own countries, something that would destroy the international mafias that thrive on illegal immigration by exploiting the despair of the migrants and the deliberate hypocrisy and absence of a vision of the various European countries that are treating migrants as if they were hot potatoes to be passed on to others.

Beyond economic misery and climate change – the two reinforce each other – geopolitics has become a serious aggravating factor in Africa. Defeated in the Middle East (particularly in Syria and Iraq), fundamentalist Islamic groups have sought refuge in the closest and weakest of continents, Africa, and in particular in its Western part, Sahel, a huge piece of land that includes countries as diverse and fragile as Mali, Burkina-Faso, Guinea, Niger, and Sudan. Benefiting from favorable conditions, but with worsening economic and climatic conditions, weak and corrupt political regimes, and resentment against the former colonial powers (France in particular), these groups have continued to progress with a little help, lately, from an opportunistic Russia and its Wagner militias. In turn, this increased insecurity and extreme poverty have aggravated a migratory phenomenon that has contributed to reinforce, in the Western world, an already negative vision of the African continent.

In return, African elites often describe the rules-based international order as having failed to serve their interests. For these critics, this order is one of oppression and not of protection. It has preserved a status quo in which major world powers (be they now Western or Eastern), have maintained their position of dominance over the Global South. These African elites are using history to illustrate their case, and they have a long list of examples to draw on. There are so many cases of unjustified rapid and brutal exploitation. In 1880, for example, the African continent was largely unexplored by Europeans. Less than thirty years later, only Liberia and Ethiopia remained unconquered by them. The rest –10 million square miles with at that time a population of 110 million people – had been carved up by five European powers in the name of the Four C's: Commerce, Christianity, Civilization, Conquest. And, in the particular case of France, the need to redress an unfavorable balance of power situation in Europe played a major role. According to the French historian Henri Brunschwig, France, after being defeated in the Franco-Prussian war (1870–1), went on to conquer Africa with eyes turned on Europe. This new empire was meant to balance the weight of a freshly unified Germany in Europe. After the "experience" of slavery starting in the sixteenth century, it was no longer the men, but the land itself and its "riches" that were – in a way – the equivalent of a gold rush. It is only natural that emotionally, if not politically, "we," the European West, should pay a price for "that," one century and a half later. As Under Secretary for the Colonies, Winston Churchill was aware of the moral difficulties the West would face one day. On January 23, 1906, he wrote the following memorandum, quoted by the British historian Thomas Pakenham in his impressive book *The Scramble for Africa*: "The chronic bloodshed which stains the West African season region is odious and disquieting. Moreover, the whole enterprise is liable to be misrepresented by persons unacquainted with imperial terminology as the murdering of natives and the stealing of their lands." Churchill may have wanted to defend the Western case, but as such his warning reads as a terrible self-indictment. What else needs to be said?

More than 100 years later, Tim Murithi, a South African professor at the University of Cape Town, goes much further in his article "Order of oppression: Africa's quest for a new international system" (*Foreign Affairs*, May/June 2023).

According to Murithi, for the greater part of the past 500 years, the international order has been explicitly designed to exploit Africa. "The transatlantic slave trade saw more than 10 million Africans kidnapped and shipped to the Americas, where their forced labor made elites in Europe and the United States exceptionally wealthy." The Arab slave trade, of course, enslaved at least as many Africans over a longer period.

How does one transcend such a past when, emotionally, the past is not past, but is still perceived as ongoing and has even intensified compared to decades ago, when decolonization offered hope? It is often said that one should not judge the past by the criteria of the present. Even if for most of our ancestors up until the second half of the eighteenth century, slavery was simply a fact of life, such a "fact of life" can never be relativized, whatever the distinctions and subtleties one wants to introduce in one's reading of history. Slavery was an absolute evil, and cannot be perceived otherwise. On that topic, historical relativism – or worse, revisionism – is simply unacceptable. In a new assessment of the West's colonial record, *Colonialism: A Moral Reckoning*, University of Oxford professor Nigel Biggar offers a moral inquest into the colonial past with the intention of contesting damaging falsehoods and thereby helping to rejuvenate faith in the West's future. I personally believe this is the wrong way to deal with the African continent and, more globally, with the Global South. To push for a different understanding of history does not advance the Western case; it does just the reverse. The central question emotionally lies elsewhere and could be formulated in the following terms. As with a mathematical formula, there is an inversely proportional relationship between resentment and confidence. With the rise of confidence, resentment may diminish. But with the decline in self-confidence, resentment explodes. You carry in you a sense of terrible injustice that you cannot transcend and that cannot be superseded. This is quite simply a recipe for disaster. And the only way to fight it is not to forget or to forgive the past, but to consciously decide that life must go on, and that it is the task of one's generation to move forward and try to succeed in spite of the weight, some would say the overweight, of the past.

In 1999, when Thabo Mbeki had just become president-elect of South Africa, I had a long private discussion with him in my office at IFRI (the French Institute for International Relations). He was about to give a conference talk that I was going to chair. It was a special day. In London, the House of Lords had just decided that British justice could indict the former president of Chile, General Pinochet, for crimes against humanity. I was very pleased with this decision and I asked Mbeki whether, today, he felt like a British lord. His answer was quick and dismissive: "Definitely not!" He went on to explain that there existed a contradiction between justice and peace. One had to transcend the past and the desire for justice in order to move forward with the present. He applied this formula to the South African case. The Rainbow Nation's early successes were, in his eyes, the product of this deliberate will to go beyond the wounds of the past. Initially, I was surprised by his answer, but then I came to accept his point of view, seeing it as the application of what could be described as the "Mandela Method." To forgive and to move forward. Today, a quarter of a century later, I am no longer sure. Forgetting may prove useful in the short run. In the long run, it is no less than a deadly poison. In South Africa, what made the peaceful end of apartheid possible was not the choice of a method, but the encounter between two exceptional men, Mandela and de Klerk (of course Mandela even more so than de Klerk), a miraculous coincidence, which was never reproduced – and clearly not on the Israel/Palestine front. (Rabin was assassinated, and Arafat was no Mandela.) It is difficult not to interpret Algeria's fixation with the past, at least in part, as the direct consequences of the country's multiple failures to deal with the present. It does not mean that France's responsibilities are not enormous and still very present. Even if one takes the most generous interpretation of French colonialism, it does nobody any good unless they are themselves involved in the process. The formula "I know what is good for you better than you do yourself" is a recipe for disaster. It proved so in Algeria, and most probably very recently in the countries of Sahel (Mali, Burkina-Faso, and Niger). Beyond the issue of Russian influence, what have the French done wrong in their approach to these countries? Why should African military elites – educated, trained, and supported by France – have turned against their "protectors" if they had not felt humiliated and treated as second-class citizens, i.e. barely, or not at all, consulted in the choice of strategy?

"I reflect for you, and you can die for me"

I used to give frequent lectures in the various military schools in France. I experienced at first hand, in relations between French and African officers, what can only be described as paternalism. "I want good things for you, but we are not in the same category." These matters are very delicate. It is so easy to humiliate someone without even being aware of it. All the more so when one does not bother to listen or to read what the "other" thinks. The situation becomes even more complex and intractable when an element of competition between Western powers adds a flavor of postcolonial nostalgia to the situation on the ground. In the case of Rwanda, which saw the terrible genocide of Tutsis by Hutus in 1994, the position of then French President François Mitterrand was in large part determined by his willingness to defend the interests of Francophone Africa from the "growing ambitions" (these were his words, as quoted by Hubert Vedrine, one of his key advisors who went on to become foreign minister under Jacques Chirac's presidency) of Anglophone Africa. After the military coup in Niger in 2023, following those that had already taken place in Mali and Burkina-Faso, one sensed also an element of competition over methods of actions and interests between Washington and Paris. It was as if the two countries were completely unaware of the arguments they were giving to the Russians, not to mention the Islamic fundamentalist groups. "Once imperialist, always imperialist." They were, so to speak, reinforcing the conviction of so many Africans for whom the so-called rules-based order of the West is downright hypocritical. On the one hand, they say, "our" illegal interventions (in Libya for example) have sowed terror across the Global South, and, on the other hand, that "we" the West have failed to intervene when it was an absolute humanitarian necessity: in Rwanda in 1994, in Srebrenica in 1995, in Sri Lanka in 2009.

This African argument is strong but not exhaustive, for it deliberately fails to see the responsibility of Africans themselves: from the civil war in Ethiopia, to the civil war in Sudan, for example. These are two completely useless conflicts that have very little to do with the West, and are mostly the product of the infectious greed of the opposing camps within the military, in the case of Sudan, or the tribal rivalries in Ethiopia. When wealth is the direct product of power, when no sense of public good really exists, when the concept of the rule of law remains totally abstract, what can one expect? Of course, greed has been tolerated if not encouraged for much too long by former colonial powers. It is probably fair to say that this culture of corruption is even more visible in Francophone than in Anglophone Africa, for reasons that up to this day remain unclear to me. The best answer is probably that, through greed, one could hope to maintain an element of control – a short-sighted strategy that proved catastrophic in the long run, but characterizes the post-immature, colonial mentality of so many of the people in charge then and maybe even now. I remember a time when defense treaties between African countries and France were being signed as French troops were landing on the airport tarmacs of various former parts of the French empire. Their aim was to restore order, or to impose a different order more favorable to French interests. Other former colonial powers had very ambivalent attitudes toward France's interventionism. In 1978, after the French intervention in Katanga, a British newspaper ran a leading article with a headline noting enviously (though I can't recall the exact words): "We used to behave just like the French." There was undoubtedly an element of admiration for what the French paratroopers had just achieved, and some nostalgia for the British imperial tradition. Much later on, in January 2013, I was participating in the annual French British encounter, known as "Le Colloque," when the French intervention in Mali was announced. Operation Serval had just begun. I remember vividly the attitude of some of the British participants, so utterly different in content from the title of *The Times* more than thirty years earlier. They came to me as if I had just had a loss in my family: "All our condolences, all our thoughts are going out to you." Two days later, after the obvious initial success of the French operation – the capital of Mali, Bamako, had not fallen into the hands of the rebels – their tone had changed completely. They were almost complimenting me, even if they did have some reservations. How could one ever dream of controlling such a huge territory with so few men? History has not proved them wrong.

Seen from Africa, European (mostly French now) military interventionism is seen as much as part of the problem as part of the solution. Terrorist groups have to be resisted, and hopefully successfully contained in Africa, after having been defeated in the Middle East. But the presence of European bases and soldiers also constitutes a card in the hands of terrorists, all the more so if there is a third totally opportunistic actor that, under the pretext of fighting terrorism, seeks above all to enrich itself and do its utmost to destabilize and ultimately defeat the West. Could Russia be seeking in Africa what France sought at the end of the nineteenth century after being defeated in the Franco-Prussian war? A new front allowing it to balance the old central one? Moscow looks at Africa today with eyes turned to Europe. If Russia cannot take control of Ukraine, the way it wanted, it can at least see in its progression in Africa something like a compensation prize. Today, we might ask ourselves whether Africa is not about to return to be what it was at the time of the Cold War, a major stake in the competition among powers. This perception seems to be shared by Washington, which, to the relief but also embarrassment of the French, is coming to their help. America welcomed France's interventionist tradition in Africa. There was an element of division of labor between the two countries that seemed to reflect Adam Smith's law of comparative advantage. Of course, there was a time when the United States condemned France's colonial presence on the African continent. As a young senator from Massachusetts, JFK (John Fitzgerald Kennedy) was particularly vocal in denouncing French colonialism in Algeria.

This renewed "scramble for Africa" should force us to consider the following question. How can one reimagine multilateralism and redesign international institutions to create a more effective global system of collective security? It is fair to say that an African vision for global order should be based on the principles of equality and the need to redress historical wrongs. Solidarity among African states and societies helped sustain the struggle against colonialism and apartheid in the twentieth century. And it is a noble project to expect that, once targets of historical injustice, Africans could become leading voices for justice, meaning fairness, equality, accountability, and redress for past harms.

At a very personal level, I still remember my father telling me he had been liberated by American soldiers on May 8, 1945, from the concentration camp he was in after Auschwitz, in Austria close to Mauthausen. He saw a powerful symbol in the fact that these soldiers were black. Descendants from slaves were the instruments of freedom for the modern-day slaves my father had become part of as a result of Hitler's madness. Of course, Blacks were not systematically extermiǹated the way Jews were, but the structural discrimination they faced over time was far stronger than in the case of the Jews. From that standpoint of suffering, Israel and the African continents should have come much closer in the postwar past. The respective victims of the Shoah and slavery should have been able to understand each other better than they did. It was not to be the case. Far from it. This "lost opportunity" was in part due to the process of the Cold War itself. Israel had to choose a camp, and chose the West. A natural and largely inevitable choice. But beyond geopolitics, Jews were perceived as Western elites, if not the ultimate incarnation of the white arrogance of success by many Black community leaders in America, and some African leaders in Africa. As for Israelis, they approached the African continent mostly with cold geopolitical eyes. Apartheid did not prevent them from continuing to sell weapons to the South African regime, even at a time when it was ostracized and subject to sanctions by the majority of Western countries.

There is obviously a danger in describing the world "as it should be" as depicted in the plays of Corneille, rather than the world "as it is" as depicted by Racine, both seventeenth-century French playwrights.

To say that African societies can show the world how to promote reconciliation between warring groups and communities, following the South African model, is also in retrospect difficult to take at face value. Since the end of apartheid in South Africa, a remarkable development for which the world owes as much to F. W. de Klerk as it does to Nelson Mandela, and internationally the end of the Cold War and the collapse of the Soviet Union, the reconciliation process has not – and this is an understatement – progressed.

Ethnic cleansing in Rwanda in 1994, wars on the Horn of Africa, in particular in Ethiopia, and civil wars in Sudan. It would be easy to question the moral legitimacy of the African countries that are urging, in the name of reconciliation and justice, a new international order based on a more balanced distribution of power. More than half of UN Security Council meetings and 70 percent of Security Council resolutions with Chapter 7 mandates – those authorizing peacekeepers to use force – concern African security issues. Yet, as is well known, no African country, and for that matter no Latin American or Middle Eastern country, is a permanent member of the UN Security Council.

For chaos does not exist only within some key African states, but also, in some cases, in the relationship between various African states. Rwanda's leader for more than two decades, Paul Kagame, is accused of sowing chaos in his neighboring country, the Democratic Republic of Congo. Is he not backing the M23 rebel group, whose members are mostly ethnic Tutsis like Kagame himself? Is Rwanda inspired by self-defense, or a spirit of revenge against the Hutus responsible for the 1994 genocide, who took refuge in the Democratic Republic of Congo? Or should Kagame's ambition be seen as the exploitation of the rancor of the past for the benefits of the present? Does he wish to assert Rwanda's dominance over its immediate neighbors and gain access to the natural resources of a vast region that is largely up for grabs since the departure of President Mobutu Sese Seko to exile in 1997. Whoever is responsible, Kagame carries more than his share, as Congo and Rwanda could well be on the brink of all-out war. And this conflict risks pulling in a growing number of African states, from Kenya to South Sudan, from Burundi to Uganda. In brief, a recipe for disaster. There was a time when Kagame and his Rwandan Patriotic Front benefited from the sympathy of the Western world. Did he not restore peace after having ended the genocide in Rwanda? And Congo, by contrast, was in chaos, a negative model for West Africa, starting with the Sahel region.

In spite of these negative evolutions, is it fair to say that Africa has simply switched emotions, moving from being the continent of hope to become the continent of despair? This would be a simplistic caricature of an evolution that is much more complex than it seems at first glance. Africa has cards that should not be condescendingly neglected.

In fact, there may be more hope at the end of the day in Africa than there is in Latin America.

Latin America still continues to disappoint

In identity terms, should one describe Latin America as the extreme West, or should one emphasize the Pacific temptations of the continent, not to mention the weight of African roots, in particular in a country like Brazil? This embarrassment of riches, of possible choice of directions, constitutes more a source of weakness than of strength.

The fact is nothing seems to change for the better in a continent that Simón Bolívar or, in his revolutionary way, Che Guevara wanted to unite. In fact, today, one wonders in a provocative manner whether the narco-dealers are not more successful at uniting the continent under the spell of terror than anyone before them. In August 2023, one of the leading candidates to the presidential elections in Ecuador was executed almost certainly on the order of drug cartels from Mexico. The continent continues to navigate between violence, misery, and populism.

The contrast with the hopes of the past remains bigger than ever. In the early 1950s, a country like Argentina was far ahead of the Republic of Korea in terms of GDP. Of course, Latin America benefited more than any other continent from World War II. One could say that Latin America was to the world what Switzerland was to Europe: a precious oasis of peace. During and after the war, places such as Havana, Buenos Aires, and Rio de Janeiro, had become places of high culture, where artists, mostly from Europe, could find places to perform or even to survive.

But the absence of a genuine external challenge such as Nazi Germany or the Soviet Union may constitute an ambivalent gift; the United States, contrary to what some pretend to be the case, represented a less dangerous challenge (is the case of Chile under Pinochet an exception, or part of a pattern of intervention in the affairs of the continent?). Precisely because one is not mobilized by the need to resist or confront the diktats or aggression of the world, one can easily lapse into a state of internal complacency, if not of total domination under a culture of corruption, and resignation to failure.

The Latin American continent's main, some would say only, hope remains its giant: Brazil. The country has found of late a new role, one that gives it a sense of a global and vital mission for the world and not only for the continent. Brazil has presented itself, since the Belen regional conference on the future of the Amazon in July 2023, as *the* leading country in the battle against climate change. Saving the Amazon from deforestation is an absolute priority if one wants to have any chance of reversing the process of global warming. This is the message that Lula, the Brazilian president, perfectly expresses. At a time when Latin America is once again perceived as the continent of violence, when Mexican drug cartels are expanding their activities and crimes to countries beyond their border, Brazil, thanks to its sense of responsibility for the planet, will redress at least in part the image of the entire continent. Men may continue to die by the bullet in frightening numbers, but trees will be protected from men's greed. This is at least the project. Will it work? That is another matter. But at a time of such crisis for the planet, with its combination of extreme temperatures, fires, and floods, there should exist less tolerance for the increasing deterioration of politics. Deterioration, which could be characterized by Javier Milei, a former journalist who presents himself as an Argentinian version of Trump in America, or of Bolsonaro in Brazil, has easily won the presidential elections – as if populism did not suffer enough from its constant and inevitable failures.

Recently, I had the opportunity to address a group of Latin American (mostly Brazilian) executives at a seminar on geopolitics at INSEAD, one of the leading management schools in the world. It was clear from the debate I had with them following my seminar that they were deeply aware of the failings of their continent. Brazilians in particular were not convinced that their country-continent was performing much better than the rest of Latin America – unlike nearly two decades earlier when their country had benefited from a long period of "rationality," as Fernando Henrique Cardoso's two terms as president were followed by Lula's first presidency. They were surprisingly modest. The Brazilian version of Donald Trump, Jair Bolsonaro, had left a negative impact on their sense of dignity and self-respect, and the beginnings of Lula's second presidency was leaving them uncertain.

Might we be witnessing something that could be described as a process of the Latin-Americanization of Brazil? Brazilians were so keen to distinguish themselves from the pack, from the rest of the continent. Because they have failed to bring the others to their level, are Brazilians, in spite of their incredible energy, of their unique resources, being pulled down by the rest of their continent? This process could be compared with the evolution of Israel in the Middle East, which I described earlier as the "Middle Easternization" of Israel.

Such interrogations, which are the product of open, liberal societies, do not exist in the second pole of our triangle, which I have denominated the Global East, in reference of course to the Global South.

3

The Hardening of the Global East

A tough and revealing debate in Singapore

January 1992. I was the guest of a prominent think-tank in Singapore. I had been assigned the task of defending the Western position on a highly topical and delicate subject: universal or Western values? Western values were presenting themselves as universal, but were they really? What if they were just Western, and being used by the West to impose their values and models on others? Just an updated version of the "Mission to Civilize" so fashionable in the nineteenth century, and so convenient for hiding the appetite of the European colonial powers for enrichment and power? After the fall of the Berlin Wall, and the publication of Francis Fukuyama's provocative article, which then became a book, *The End of History*, Asia, and particularly Singapore, was on the defensive. Singapore is a bridge between civilizations, the only Asian country also to have a Museum of Asian Art, in fact maybe the only country in the region to consider itself truly Asian, a word created by the West and not shared by the immense majority of the inhabitants of that geographic zone. Chinese are Chinese, Japanese are Japanese, Indonesians are Indonesian. Singapore was above all the living proof that enlightened despotism could be a successful formula and model outside the democratic world, and that political culture should not be confused with culture, or the rule of law with democracy. Following the imperialist values of the first half of the century, the triumphalism of the democratic West, as trumpeted by Francis Fukuyama, could only be perceived in Singapore as an anachronistic attempt to return to the past, under the mask of a model that had its roots in ancient Greece: a world that had very little, if anything, in common with Southeast Asia.

When I accepted the invitation, I could not suspect that my presentation would take place just a few weeks after the suspension of the electoral process in Algeria. The FIS (Islamic Salvation Front) had won the first ballot with a clear majority; the Algerian army, in control of power, did not allow the second round to take place. This total breach of democracy was met in Paris with a resounding silence that could be equated with support. My friends and colleagues in Singapore, who had been for years irritated by my democratic zeal, were only too happy to seize on the event, to denounce the "hypocrisy of the West." The defense of democracy was sacred as long as the results of the electoral process satisfied "us, the West," they told me. What could I answer? Was the position of France defensible in terms of values and principles? A bloody civil war ensued as the result of this suspension of the democratic process.

The Algerian people had expressed itself with the utmost clarity. Seizing on the old motto of the French Revolution, I tried my luck with Saint-Just's formula: "There is no Freedom for the enemies of Freedom." It did not satisfy my interlocutors. They were not interested in the French Revolution; they felt closer to the Enlightened despotism that had preceded the revolution in the rest of continental Europe. Frederick the Great of Prussia and Catherine the Great of Russia were maybe distant and vague references for them; Saint-Just meant nothing at all. I pursued my intellectual counteroffensive by referring to the concept of universal values and respect for life, which I explained was a clearer priority at the end of the twentieth century in the West, less so in Asia. The death penalty had been abolished in France eleven years earlier, whereas it still existed in Singapore (and exists to this day and is applied also to women). They were still not convinced, and proceeded to lecture me on the need for the Western world to accept and respect Asian values. Meritocracy was in their eyes perhaps an even better formula than democracy in order to rule a country efficiently, especially if it was accompanied, like in Singapore and unlike in China, by the rule of law. Most of my interlocutors in the room were of Chinese descent. They saw themselves as proof of the success of the fusion between a training in the best Western universities, mostly American and British, and the Mandarinate tradition (combining thereby openness and extreme sophistication). They added further that my Western emphasis on the value of life seemed shallow, since it was not accompanied by Asia's traditional respect for the elderly.

More than three decades later, I still have a vivid memory of this very frank (in the language of diplomacy) exchange. I felt like a punchbag, or, to put it more elegantly if my origins allow such a comparison, like Saint Sebastian, pierced by intellectual arrows. I felt also very cold (because of the air conditioning) and above all very lonely. The French ambassador who had organized the debate, and was present in the room, did not think it appropriate to intervene in the exchange. (He went on to occupy very prestigious positions in the French diplomatic cursus, and we became, and still are, very good friends).

What struck me in this particular debate in Singapore was the confidence of my Asian hosts. In their eyes, and that was already more than thirty years ago, we had no lessons to teach them either in terms of morality or in terms of efficiency. They had their own model and were convinced it was the right one for them (if not for the world one day). This highly combative and intense moment, in terms of values and models, remained imbued with exquisite courtesy. My interlocutors were vehement, but remained cordial. In retrospect, this moment, I now see, contained a prefiguration of the new world in which we have entered. One in which authoritarian countries not only resist the West, but intend to substitute our *Weltanschauung* (world vision) for theirs. They are increasingly convinced that "our" time had passed, and that "their" time has finally arrived.

In 1992, images of the tanks in Tiananmen Square were still very present and Russia seemed to be tentatively heading toward a form of democracy (even if a chaotic one). America seemed at the helm of a unipolar moment. Yet, this debate on values was a warning of things to come: the fragility of the Western argument I was defending, the combination of resentment and confidence expressed by my hosts in Singapore. Substitute Singapore with China, and what I experienced in 1992 was an eye opener into the future, i.e. the present we live in today.

The arguments that were used, in an intellectually strong, yet moderate, manner by Singapore's elites are now used in a much more brutal manner by the Chinese. However, it is important to stress that the leaders of the City Island whose predecessors were tackling me in 1992 (some of whom still occupy high positions) perceive today's China, as it has evolved under Xi Jinping, more as a bully than as a glorious incarnation of their own model. Chinese civilization was a source of pride and inspiration, but Chinese reality today is a threat, especially for its Asian neighbors, and could well become ideologically a source of embarrassment.

The rise of the Global East

The expression "Global East" is not commonly used. By Global East, I am referring to the group of countries that are animated by a revisionist vision of the world, that are not afraid to use force, both outside to enlarge or recuperate territories they deem to belong to them and inside to crush any kind of dissent. In this definition of the Global East, geography matters very little. It would be wrong to reduce the definition of the Global South to economics, restricting it to the poor or barely emerging countries. Saudi Arabia is a key actor of the Global South and a very wealthy one. In the case of the Global East, the economy matters little. What prevails, as we will see later, is a combination of ardent nationalism and deeply anti-democratic and anti-Western ideologies. I am creating the category (not having found other references to it) as a counterpart to the now commonly used term "Global South." In fact, there is an element of competition (if not confusion) between the two global groups (East and South), since some key members of what I describe as the Global East perceive themselves (and want to be perceived) as part of the Global South – as if the latter term were far more attractive than the first, at least in terms of soft power. The most prominent country figuring in the two groups is of course China. But beyond these two groups, there is a third entity based on the BRICS acronym (Brazil, Russia, India, China, joined later on by South Africa) invented as early as 2001 by a British economist from Goldman Sachs, Jim O'Neill. It was an astute marketing idea that was institutionalized in 2011, and one that Beijing intends to enlarge. In 2023, six new countries were invited to join the BRICS: Saudi Arabia, Iran, Ethiopia, Egypt, the United Arab Emirates, and Argentina – five new members from the Middle East and one from Latin America. The idea behind the enlargement of BRICS, pushed by Beijing, is to reshuffle the world order, by turning it into an alternative to the G20, whose relatively pro-Western (if not democratic) bias is opposed by China. But there is a major caveat in the Chinese project. India, another prominent member of BRICS, sees China as its main rival, if not the most direct threat to its security. Delhi needs Washington to balance Beijing and (as we have seen earlier in the previous chapter) is not ready to make a clear choice between the two camps. China may present itself as belonging both in the East and the South. Today's India thinks of itself as belonging to the South, but *not* to the East. As for Russia, it clearly is East but not South. That is, unless one defines the South in strict economic terms, singling out poverty, low productivity growth; unless one emphasizes also the life expectancy of its male population – a little over 60 – which led Russia to be described as a "white Africa." In fact, some demographers estimate today that the life expectancy of Russian men is shorter than that of the average African male.

How to define precisely the Global East?

The Global East can be identified by three main characteristics: anger, growing asymmetry, civilizational contest. One cannot help but notice that members of the Global East constitute the main source of danger in their respective regional zones: Russia for Europe, Iran for the Middle East, North Korea (if not increasingly China) for Asia.

The first characteristic of the Global East is its anger toward the Global West. The styles of opposition may differ, but the negative emotions and intentions are there. This club of hardcore opponents to Western values and Western interests brings together countries as diverse as China, Russia, and North Korea. And one should also include countries such as Iran, Nicaragua, and Cuba, not to mention other pariah states such as Myanmar. Belarus belongs naturally to the club, but can no longer be considered as an independent state. It has been fully vassalized by Russia. All these countries not only have in common their hostility to the West and its liberal democratic model; they are also incredibly tone deaf to the notion of the law, in spite of the apparent legalism in their practice of despotism. In fact, they ignore the meaning of the rule of law, as if strict respect for the law were a concept from another planet.

They also share in various degrees a common characteristic: in these countries, the state has effectively destroyed civil society (if it ever existed before, which is dubious in countries such as North Korea) and the fundamentals of citizenship. They have attempted to do so with a growing degree of success. North Korea used to be seen as an extremely baroque case: a sect more than a nation. But the recent evolution of Putin's Russia, or even Xi Jinping's China, has turned Pyongyang into an acceptable ally rather than an extreme caricature, which is what it remains for the Western world. A caricature, with an armored train, but also, potentially, nuclear weapons. North Korea may remain a shrewd "Mad House," blackmailing the world with its nuclear weapons in order to survive in infamous isolation. But it is becoming a possible prefiguration of how Iran would behave, should that country attain its nuclear ambitions. A prospect that seems to be getting closer.

Beyond anger toward the West, the second characteristic of the Global East is the growing asymmetry between its core members. With an ever stronger China – whatever its present economic difficulties – and an ever weaker Russia. The great beneficiary from the second Iraq war in 2003 was Iran. Could historians conclude in the future that China was the great beneficiary of the war in Ukraine, turning that war into a huge distraction for the West and an armed struggle among European nations? It would come as a natural conclusion if China were to use the present conflict in Europe (not to mention the near political chaos in America) to further its interests in Asia through military and other means.

To say that China has – since the end of the Soviet Union – exchanged roles with Russia, ultimately replacing that country as senior partner, misses the essential point. Beijing and Russia – whatever the desperate demonstrations of force by Moscow – are no longer boxing in the same category. And they are not treated in the same way by the Western world, which would probably have been much more prudent toward Beijing than it has been toward Moscow had China behaved as aggressively in the South China Sea as Russia in Ukraine. For the West needs China much more than it needs Russia. And China, though it may want the war in Ukraine to drag on, and continues to help Russia militarily, technologically, and above all economically, does not want it to escalate out of control. Can one go as far as to suggest that China is on course to vassalize Russia, in a way that Russia has failed to vassalize Ukraine? It may very well be so, given the low level of respect the Chinese have traditionally had for the Russians, whatever the proclaimed friendship between the respective current leaders of the two countries.

The third characteristic that unites the key countries of the Global East is their emphasis on the "civilizational nature" of their struggle against the West. Listening to the respective speeches of the leaders of China and Russia, one would be tempted to conclude: "Samuel Huntington, Vladimir Putin, and Xi Jinping: same struggle." But that would be a superficial conclusion. In fact, with the benefits of hindsight, one can only conclude that Huntington, in his famous *Clash of Civilizations* (first published as an article in *Foreign Affairs* in 1993 and then as a book in 1996), was wrong. In his essay, he described the world as a succession of struggles. The clash of nationalism had begun with the French Revolution in 1789, the clash of ideologies with the Russian revolution in 1917. The collapse of the Soviet Union in 1991, following the fall of the Berlin Wall, had not brought about the "end of history" as announced prematurely by Francis Fukuyama, but the return of the good old clash of civilizations of ancient times. Confusing culture and political culture, Huntington failed to see the different and more complex reality that describes best our present-day world. What we are witnessing is the superimposition of different layers of clashes often hidden under a civilizational disguise. If one takes China and Russia, both have experienced with a vengeance the return of a clash of ideologies with the West. Civilizational and ideological layers are superseded in both cases by a strong and aggressive dose of nationalism based on a rewriting of history: more caricatural in Russia, more subtle in China. But the results are the same. "We can only triumph in Ukraine because we are the inheritors of those who won in the Great Patriotic War" (World War II), says Putin in an act of defiance that completely suppresses the two years of the German/Soviet pact between 1939 and 1941. Two years of cynical infamy that underscored the true nature of the Soviet Regime under Stalin. In the Chinese case, the sense of superiority seems to be based less on results and performances than on essence. Never forget, say the Chinese, we are the inheritors of the greatest civilization on earth. Until the end of the eighteenth century, we were the number one power in the world. Up until 1815, we were the number one producer of manufactured goods in the world. We are logically, irresistibly, and legitimately returning to be what we were: the number one power in the world.

The greater the frustrations with the present, both in China and Russia, the more urgent it is to use the past to redress the balance of emotions that may exist within their respective national storytelling. "I can't make you rich (any longer in the Chinese case), I don't want to make you free – it would be a dangerous Western-style temptation that has nothing to do with who we are – but I can and I will make you proud, for we are going to successfully resist Western aggression and show the decaying West the superiority of our respective civilizations."

China's uncertain return to primacy

In the opening pages of his book *On China*, Henry Kissinger evokes, with a mixture of admiration and bewilderment, the meeting that took place in Beijing in 1961 between Chairman Mao and his key generals. We were on the eve of war with

India, one of many, over the Himalaya. "We are going to proceed as China did under the Tang dynasty (618/907)," says Mao. "We enter with all our forces and once our objectives are attained, we withdraw immediately." In his early years, Kissinger had dreamt of introducing Europe's diplomatic sophistication into the United States. He ended up celebrating China's long-term strategic visions, backed by a deliberate use of the past as model. The United States had no clear plan to withdraw from Vietnam once they became involved, and democratic impediments prevented America from operating a functional and sophisticated diplomacy.

Attending a debate with Angela Merkel in Beijing

What I experienced personally in Beijing in the winter of 2015 was of a totally different nature. Kissinger may have been fascinated by the sophistication of Chinese diplomacy – was he paying tribute to the Chinese or to himself, who had been a key actor in the opening of the United States to the Middle Kingdom? – but the debate I attended between the German Chancellor Angela Merkel and the leaders of the International Relations Committee of the Chinese Communist Party (CCP) gave me a totally different impression. I was the guest of an important German foundation, and my friendship with its president, who had once been president of the German Federal Republic, gave me, a non-German, this privileged access. The exchange was "frank," to use the diplomatic expression. To go to the essence of the meeting, the Chinese were trying to divide Germans (and beyond them the Europeans) and Americans. "How can you trust a country that has been spying on you by getting access to your mobile phone?" the Chinese immediately asked Angela Merkel. The conversation took place in the aftermath of the revelation of the Pegasus scandal. How could President Barack Obama have authorized such a total breach of confidence? If Washington can allow this lack of civility to occur between such close allies, how could one trust Americans? Merkel was unmoved. She replied by emphasizing the depth and importance of the longstanding and close friendship between Berlin and Washington. One should not confuse regrettable but minor incidents with fundamental long-term trends. It was the chancellor's turn to address the Chinese delegation. She stressed: "You insist on your role at the United Nations and you proclaim at every opportunity the importance you attach to it (and the money you spend for the UN). But in reality, you concentrate your energy in Asia, scaring your neighbors in the process. Should you not be doing the reverse? Contribute more to the security of Africa and the Middle East for example?" And she concluded: "You need to balance your priorities if you want to be recognized as a positive international actor, working for the common good of the planet."

A few months later, at an informal Franco-Chinese lunch in Paris, a Chinese delegate had an interesting answer to Angela Merkel's question: "We cannot take risks with the lives of our soldiers in conflicts that do not fully concern us, given the nature of our One Child Policy. Only children's lives cannot be risked in Africa or the Middle East." When I reported that story to a well-known French specialist of China, he was not impressed, or convinced. In his eyes, it was nothing more than a propaganda trick. The Chinese delegation in Beijing seemed surprised by the combative tone of the German chancellor. They had treated her as a star. The Beijing sky was exceptionally blue during the days she was there. My German friends explained to me that the clouds had been artificially dispersed, the polluting factories closed for the duration of her visit. When he arrived in Beijing just a few days later, French President François Hollande did not get such royal treatment. He had failed to cultivate his links with China. It was his first visit after more than three years as president, and the official trip lasted no more than two days. What could he expect? Angela Merkel had traveled to China twice a year since she had become Chancellor. Obviously, the trade links between Germany and China were far more important than those between Paris and Beijing. At that time, Germany's Chinese policy – reflecting the overall global ambition of the Europeans – could be summarized quite plainly: maximize trade, minimize economic and geopolitical risks, make reference to human rights as little as possible or only when absolutely necessary.

The Xi Jinping moment

The debate I attended in Beijing with Angela Merkel took place a decade ago. Since then, Xi Jinping has managed to consolidate his power at the head of the CCP and to secure an unprecedented third term. The former prime minister and foreign minister of Australia, Kevin Rudd, a long-time specialist of China, has spent three years at Oxford University writing a DPhil thesis dedicated to the worldview of Xi Jinping and his ambitions for China. Rudd's conclusions are worrisome to say the least. For him, the rise of Xi has meant "nothing less than the return of the ideological man" in China. We had been told at the end of the twentieth century that the twenty-first century would probably be dominated by religious clashes and would definitely be post-ideological. China has demonstrated the total opposite. The majority of the world defines itself vis-à-vis, if not in stark opposition to, Western views and values (Russia included). This is not the case with China. The Chinese see the world through their own eyes, blending, in the case of Xi Jinping, ideological purity with technocratic pragmatism. As Rudd reminds us, Xi Jinping bases his thinking on historical and dialectical materialism. Deng Xiaoping gave priority to economic reforms over political ones, convinced that the Russian path chosen by Gorbachev was dangerous. Thirty years later, Xi Jinping goes, with hindsight, much further. He seems convinced that ideological decay led to the collapse of Soviet communism. For him, a strong ideology is the only way to crush all forms of dissent within China and to resist the West's attempt to foment ideological divisions. Marxism-Leninism also has the great advantage of placing China on the right side of history. For Xi, the real "end of history" is not the victory of liberal classical democracy, but the collapse of the United States in on itself, victims of its own internal contradictions and the inevitability of capitalist decline. In some ways, one might be tempted to say that, under Xi, China applies to America the theories used by Washington to prepare for the inevitable decline of the Soviet Union. There is a notable difference though: Xi seems in much more of a hurry than George Kennan was when he outlined his containment theory. One key reason is of an emotional nature. America was never humiliated by the East, in contrast with China, which still resents being humiliated by the West.

A conversation with Lee Kuan Yew on China

Ideology is also back with a vengeance on the economic level, as if the lessons once given by Lee Kuan Yew, founder of Singapore's miracle, had been forgotten. In 2008, Lee Kuan Yew invited me to visit him in his private mansion in the city-island. We had a very long conversation on the respective merits of the various political models. He was keen to tell me a story of which he was very proud: the first visit made to Singapore by Deng Xiaoping as the new leader of China in 1978, when he was on his way to peace negotiations on the fate of Cambodia. The first question Deng asked Lee was: "How did you make it, how did you attain such a success?" Deng had known Singapore in the early 1920s when it was just a poor peninsula infected by mosquitoes and invaded by tigers. What he had seen on his short trip from the airport to Lee's official residence had simply amazed him. There had been such stark and rapid progress since the independence of the city-state in

1965, just thirteen years earlier. Lee's short answer was summarized in one single word "Capitalism." He told me this with a discreet smile and a sense of intense pride: he saw himself as the direct father of the Chinese miracle. What would he be thinking today, now that economic growth no longer seems to be China's priority?

Xi Jinping, more than forty-five years after Deng's visit to Singapore, has set China on a radically different path. He seems to have lost confidence in the market following the global financial crisis of 2008 and the burst of a stock market bubble that in 2015 led to a nearly 50 percent collapse in the value of Chinese stocks. China had gone too far in the direction of state capitalism. The balance had to be redressed. "More state, less capitalism" could be the new Chinese motto. For Xi, through adherence to stricter Marxist principles, China would achieve national greatness and greater economic equality much more rapidly. But giving the state a greater role in controlling the economy is not necessarily a recipe for success, or a boost to confidence, especially when demography becomes problematic. When they were not allowed to have more than one child, most Chinese wanted to break that rigid rule. Now that they are encouraged to have more children, they do not rush to comply, as if they are not sure what the future holds for them.

Yet nothing would be more dangerous than to prematurely "bury" China or to consider its path to number one status in the world to be out of the question.

To be prudently realistic, when considering the present evolution of China, one has to counter two exaggerated beliefs. The first is seeing China as having entered a global Great Leap Backward. The situation of the Chinese economy is in fact much more nuanced and shows real strengths in key fields vital for the future, such as electric cars, solar energies, and artificial intelligence.

The second is the belief that China will have to redress the failing course of her economy by moving back to capitalism, if not to a liberal economy; that the present Marxist "parenthesis" will accelerate China's inevitable path toward liberalism. This vision constitutes a profound misunderstanding of the direction toward which China is really heading: a new statist economic orthodoxy.

Could China become today what Germany was on the eve of World War I?

The rigid, ideological, and economic path chosen by Xi is accompanied – reinforced, would be a more precise expression – by a new assertiveness in the realm of foreign policy. I remember the time when a Chinese friend, in a high position in Beijing, asked me at the World Economic Forum in Davos in 2000 how I could interpret the fact that he had been asked to prepare a report for the highest authorities of his country on the evolution of German foreign policy between 1870 and 1914, between Bismarck and Wilhelm II. My answer was immediate: "Was China going to continue to privilege caution, risk aversion, and a sense of time, the way Bismarck acted in Europe, after the unification of Germany had made of his country the strongest nation on the Continent? Or would China move toward a greater assertiveness abroad, the path chosen by Wilhelm II?" For years I had felt certain that a confident China, which had in its collective memory the sense of its greatness and was convinced it was on course quietly and slowly to return to being the number one country in the world, would prevail over a more restless one. I felt at that time that no comparison was possible between Germany on the eve of World War I and China in the first quarter of the twentieth century. But I was wrong, or, more precisely, Xi Jinping proved me wrong. For China under Xi Jinping has come to act the way Germany did in the years that preceded World War I. This does not mean that history will inevitably repeat itself, and that war is coming to the South China Sea. The optimistic scenario is that the Chinese are sufficiently aware of history not to fall into its trap. The pessimistic scenario is that the combination of Marxism, socialist ideology, and ultra-nationalism will necessarily bring a rising China and a declining America into confrontation. The key component of Chinese nationalism may be of an emotional nature. As early as 2013, Xi alludes to the importance of nationalism: "In the West there are people who say that China should change the angle of its historical propaganda, it should no longer make propaganda about its history of humiliation." And he adds: "But as I see it, we cannot heed this; forgetting history means betrayal." For Xi, "the road to rejuvenation" implies never forgetting the perfidy of the Western imperial powers and Japan and the party's heroic response during China's "100 years of national humiliation." This goes with a new reshaping of historical memory, which includes a revisionist reading of China's role in World War II, in which China is not only a victim but also an actor, and an important one even in Asia. It marks an important shift in Chinese nationalism, which often presented China more as a pure victim than as a victor. It is true that the Chinese leader who sat next to Roosevelt and Churchill at the 1943 Cairo Conference was the nationalist Chiang Kai-shek and not the communist Mao. By presenting China as a key wartime partner of the allies and a cofounder of the postwar order, the Chinese leadership seeks to suggest that China plays a similarly cooperative role in today's international community. This is a discourse that, as far as historical revisionism is concerned, is much less troubling and aggressive than Russian revisionism, but that has nevertheless little to do with historical reality, and is in sharp contrast with the ideological return to the Mao period.

In China's desire to become the key Asian and global power by 2049 for the celebration of the centenary of the CCP's rise to power, a number of quantitative benchmarks have to be reached, from the development of the economy to the modernization of China's national defense, all of this leading to a new international balance of forces, starting with "a Chinese Nation, that stands tall and firm in the East." This is already the case, at least in large part. But it is visibly not enough for Xi. A more ambitious, more aggressive China has also resorted to a new ethos, through "a wolf warrior" diplomacy. In its goal to build a fairer and more just international system, China should not chastise itself; the country is more than entitled to provide the world with an alternative model of development away from the Washington Consensus. In distancing itself from the G20, over which it has no control, and in supporting an enlarged BRICS that it dreams of leading, China intends to deepen its building of China-centric international institutions, such as the Belt and Road Initiative, the Asian Infrastructure Investment Bank, and the Shanghai Cooperation Organization.

Could China be its own worst enemy?

Is Xi's message that China is much more powerful than ever, and intends to use this power to change the course of history, shared by the Chinese people? Have they completely overcome the extreme hardships of the Mao years? And are they ready to exchange relative prosperity for rising pride and power? The answer in fact is probably "yes." And this is, above all, because the Chinese population has no real alternatives. With its new and highly sophisticated surveillance technology, the regime can control its population in ways Mao and Stalin could not have dreamt of. And fewer of the new Chinese elites have been educated abroad in prestigious universities than the generation that preceded them in the 1990s and 2000s. They are therefore even more nationalistic than their predecessors.

"It's the economy stupid." This expression, coined to focus campaigners' energies during Bill Clinton's campaign to unseat George H. W. Bush in 1992 in spite of America's recent victory in the first Gulf War in 1991, not to mention the collapse of the Soviet Union, could well apply to the future of China. The Achilles heel of Xi Jinping is the economy. As the quest for common prosperity is likely to shrink over time, long-term structural problems will take their toll. With an aging population, a shrinking workforce, low productivity growth, and high levels of debt shared between state and private financial institutions, China has objective weaknesses. And the dream of the poorest in the poorest of continents (Africa) is not to reach China, but to go to Europe, not only for obvious objective reasons, such as geographical distance, but also for more subjective ones. Non-Chinese do not seek to join a China that they do not perceive as a dream, or even as the country/continent of the future. In its quest to become the number one power in the world, is China missing fundamental points? The first may simply be the Chinese language. English (or French) are (or were) at some point universal languages. Without wanting to sound like an arrogant Westerner, can China's impenetrable language and culture be perceived as universal, especially when her population is seriously shrinking?

A question arises that is fundamental for the future balance of forces in Asia and in the world. Has China reached its peak, unlike India, and has the Middle Kingdom already started to decline? In terms of realities as well as perceptions, this is a key question. Are the Chinese entirely correct when they emphasize the huge differences that exist between them and the Russians? What if the two countries – victims of their respective ideological evolutions – were at various levels of decline? A nascent one in China, a much more advanced (matured) one in Russia?

Even if there are elements of truth in these declinist comments, the essential truth lies elsewhere. In spite of the fact it cannot keep rising eternally, China remains by far the greatest challenge the United States has had to face since it came to dominate geopolitics nearly a century ago. It's the most politically and ideologically disciplined challenger (unlike Russia or Islamic fundamentalists). It is also the one that most deeply believes in its own ideology. Using humiliation as a weapon, China has a dual revenge to exert: against Western imperialism and sense of superiority as a civilization, and against Western ideology and its conviction that it won the ideological contest in the twenty-first century. Now, they say, is the "Chinese moment": in terms of power, but also in terms of ideas and models.

The central question can be summarized as follows: will China follow Russia in its choice of war as the "continuation of politics through other means"? This is the conviction of Harvard Professor Graham Allison, in his book *Destined for War*, in which he emphasizes the recurrence in history of what he refers to as "the Thucydides Trap." A rising power and a declining power like Sparta and Athens in Ancient Greece are destined to confront each other militarily. But there is something too mechanistic in Allison's scheme. China is not Sparta and America is not Athens. Nuclear weapons did not exist in Ancient Greece, nor did globalization. It remains to be said that war is possible, but not inevitable. From that standpoint, the war in Ukraine is more a warning than an encouragement for the Chinese. Are Russians doing that well? Young Chinese are probably more nationalistic than their parents and grandparents were. They have not experienced a cycle of war in their lifetime. But there are significant differences between Russia and China, between Putin and Xi Jinping. I still have in mind the rather derogatory comment one of my old Davos Chinese friends who confided to me, in the early days of the war in Ukraine: "The Russians are living in the past, that's all they have. We Chinese live in the present and in the future, because we can afford to do so."

China like the United States is a global power, the number two economy in the world, if not the number one in key areas such as international trade. Russia is a unidimensional great military power and, given its performances on the battlefields of Ukraine, it is not even clear it deserves such a status. Civil society and public opinion are concepts without much reality in Russia. The Chinese, instead, are wary of their centralized authoritarian state; as we saw during the COVID period, citizens are able to establish something resembling a protest movement. Chinese power was forced to move, and certainly too quickly, from total control of society, to openness when it realized that the population could no longer accept the restrictions. Beyond having to heed such emotional uprisings from segments of the public, the Chinese leadership – which in general does not pay too much attention to the demands of society – cannot totally ignore the concerns of its economic elites and in particular the worries of the very rich. It would be a grave misunderstanding of the way China works to believe there is something like a division of power between the increasingly ideological political authorities and their economic counterparts. Xi Jinping has used the argument, or alibi, of the struggle against corruption to neutralize his opponents, whether potential or real, within the political or economic apparatus. Power has never been more centralized in China since Mao's time. Nevertheless, from conversations with Chinese friends in the course of the past few years and in particular since the hardening of Xi's policies and discourses, I could detect something like a growing irritation, if not clear-cut criticisms, of the directions taken by the present power in China. Of course, the regime is not about to fall. And China, even with a declining population and much more reduced economic growth, will remain a considerable force. But in the long run, the new statist orientation of the regime can only have a negative impact on the country's creativity and inventiveness. By centralizing itself in this way, is China giving America a final chance to redeem itself? Or, more negatively, should one speak of an inevitable competitive decay between a too centralized China and a too polarized America? That would mean new opportunities could be given to India and the European Union to play a significant role in a new multipolar world.

Could China destroy itself, the way it has "destroyed" Hong Kong? There was a time in the early 1990s when many analysts were dreaming of what they described as the "Hong-Kongization," if not "Taiwainization," of China. Capitalism leading to individualism and then to democracy. That was an illusion. One speaks today by contrast of the "Japanization" of China, meaning China is faced with a structural crisis that can only be compared with the one known by Japan since 1989. A crisis that has an important real-estate dimension: in China, there are too many empty buildings.

The last governor of Hong Kong, Christopher Patten, had few illusions about the willingness of the Chinese to respect in the long term the agreements it signed with the UK. I was his guest in Hong Kong one year before it was handed over to China. Patten did not openly share his own foreboding then. But when he returned home, he did start to voice his concerns. China would not respect its engagement to apply a One State/ Two Systems formula. That was not in the Chinese DNA; above all, that was not in the nature of the communist system. For the Chinese could well apply the formula that summarized so well the behavior of the Soviet Union during the Cold War: "What is mine is mine, what is yours (or in this particular case, what has been yours) is negotiable."

It remains to be said that whatever its contradictions and difficulties, China has potentially the means to achieve its global ambition. This is not yet the case for India, and is no longer the case for Russia.

Russia's path toward chaos

"In Europe we are hangers-on and slaves, but in Asia we are masters," once wrote Dostoyevsky, as quoted by Sergei Medvedev in his powerful 2023 book *A War Made in Russia*.

It is tempting to see Putin's quarter of a century at the helm of Russia as the third act of a slow imperial collapse that began in 1917 with the October Revolution, which resumed in 1991 with the collapse of the Soviet Union, and which could be entering its final stage with the war of choice in Ukraine. Sergei Medvedev emphasizes the contrast that has always existed between the external appearance of Russia's imperial power – vast swathes of territory, cathedrals, palaces, high culture, the atomic bomb, and space exploration (recent attempts by Russia to launch a vessel to the moon, Luna 25, on August 19, 2023, resulted in a humiliating failure, in contrast to the success of India's venture Vikram four days later) – and the inside reality, what the world does not see: slavery, boorishness, theft, lies, tyranny, and the inescapable cruelty of Russian life. How can a country that is not at peace with itself and its history be at peace with its neighbors? One can see Russia's imperial quest as a supreme form of escapism. By continuing to enlarge itself, in spite of the fact it already rules over more territories than it can control, Russia fails to confront questions for which it has no answer: who am I, a European or an Asian power? Where does my future lie, in the West or in the East? In economic terms, the expression "too big to fail" is often used to describe the persistence of major industrial or financial institutions. Could the reverse be said of Russia? An empire too big for its own good, too big to succeed? And to its objective problems, such as size, one must add subjective ones, incarnated in Russia's choices of her political models. Under Putin, Russia seems to have returned to sheer and simple "Oriental Despotism."

Has Russia known other systems? At least in appearance, supreme rulers such as Peter the Great, Catherine the Great, or even marginally Alexander I, appeared as variations of Europe's "enlightened despots" surrounding themselves with Dutch artisans, French philosophers, Italian architects, and German musicians. In the portraits made by Ilya Repin of early twentieth-century statesmen such as Sergei Witte, one sees intimations of another, more positive evolution toward responsibility, modernity, and openness. But the Russo-Japanese War, followed less than ten years later by World War I, reduced these fragile hopes to ashes. The optimism, enthusiasm even, that followed the October Revolution and the victory in the Great Patriotic War were marred by the natural despotic and cruel instinct of the winners. I remember my first visit to Russia in 1981. The people I encountered reminded me irresistibly of the character of Privy Councilor Mikulin, one of the heroes of Joseph Conrad's masterly novel *Under Western Eyes*. Totally cynical persons who gave the impression they had no emotions, ready to spill the blood of others, a blood that did not seem to be running through their veins.

A dream that became reality

In 1986, I represented IFRI at the bi-annual meeting of heads of their respective foreign affairs think-tanks. The meeting was taking place in Vienna. Inspired by an exhibition I had just seen of the Viennese secession movement, I launched myself into a presentation of the inevitable changes that were about to take place in Central and Eastern Europe. Could secession mean withdrawal of the countries of Central and Eastern Europe, which were all represented there, from the Soviet Union and the Warsaw Pact? My musings were met with indulgence. They could not prevent an original and very non-representative romantic Frenchman (in the field of international relations, the two last words sounded like an oxymoron) from expressing himself. The conference ended with a dinner in a small restaurant in the hills surrounding Vienna. We might easily have been enjoying a Schubertiade evening, if it were not for the participants themselves. But with the help of the exquisite Austrian white wines, the atmosphere became cordial. The representative of the Soviet Union, Yevgeni Primakov, raised his glass to his French colleague, "a man," he stated jokingly, "who believed in democracy." Then turning to me directly, he asked, "You believe in democracy don't you?" as if, in 1986, this was almost unimaginable. He hugged me strongly in his arms. For a moment I was afraid he would kiss me "the Russian/Soviet way" on the lips. Was he enjoying my naivety or respecting my sincerity? I would never know. As a top KGB man, Primakov was more aware than anyone of the reality of the Soviet situation, especially so soon after the Chernobyl disaster. Sometimes described as the "Russian Kissinger," he had the reputation of being a moderate.

What I know is that secession in the political (not artistic) meaning of the term was effectively about to take place. It was realistic to appear naive. A little more than three years after that dinner in the hills of Vienna, the Berlin Wall fell. A decade later, between 1996 and 1998, Yevgeny Primakov would occupy an important position as Russia's foreign minister.

The Soviet Union would barely survive the fall of the Berlin Wall, collapsing itself two years later, on December 26, 1991. And in 1991, I would meet a remarkable woman whose dream and incredible energy would change forever my perception and understanding of Russia. Lena Nemirovskaya and her husband the philosopher Iouri Senokosov wanted to open the members of the Duma (the Russian parliament) to the fundamentals of the rule of law and liberal democracy. "I too had a dream," to use Martin Luther King Jr.'s beautiful expression. I saw the young elites who attended "Lena's school" as the modern Russian equivalent of the young generals of the French Revolution. Carried forward by their energy, enthusiasm, and optimistic vision of the future, they would succeed where so many generations of liberals had failed before them: in 1825 under the reign of Nicolas I, in 1905 before the start of the Russo-Japanese war, and in 1917 at the time of the Menshevik revolution, before the Bolsheviks took over. For months, for years, their dreams were my dreams. I was recreating a link between my Russian/Jewish roots and my present. I, the son of an Auschwitz survivor, was completing my dedication to the path of reconciliation. After having participated in the reinforcement of the Franco/German reconciliation process, I was to play a role, on the margins of course, in the process of reconciliation between the Russians themselves. In retrospect, I do not think I was ever so far removed from reality, with the exception maybe of my Middle Eastern dreams of peace and reconciliation between Israelis and Palestinians.

A dream that turned into nightmare

I was missing an essential point. Even after the demise of the Soviet Union, it proved impossible for Russian society to move beyond its culture of silence, its destructive inertia, if not its dark narcissism, the conviction that in the end things cannot turn out right, that if political revolution were to happen, it could never be the "velvet" way, as in Prague in 1989. In a piece published in October 1957 in *Foreign Affairs*, "The silence in Russian culture," the British philosopher and intellectual historian Isaiah Berlin, who had spent his childhood in Russia, considered the nature of Soviet rule. What he wrote then is more than worthwhile quoting to understand the present: "Soviet society is organized not for happiness, comfort, liberty, justice, personal relationships, but for combat. Whether they wish it or not, the drivers and controllers of this immense train cannot now halt it or leap from it in mid-course, without risk of destruction. If they are to survive and above all remain in power, they must go on." Nothing has changed, nothing could change since Berlin wrote these lines. In his book *My Life as a Russian Novel*, dedicated in part to a search into the roots of his family, the French novelist Emmanuel Carrère (son of the French Academician and famous Russia specialist Hélène Carrère d'Encausse) – one might find his analysis and intuitions more exact and more profound than those of his mother – describes the abject poverty in which significant segments of Russian society live, far away from Moscow and Saint Petersburg – the very people who serve as cannon fodder for Putin's adventure in Ukraine. This may help explain the political apathy of the Russians. When your primary goal in life is to survive economically, if not physically, you are less keen for a political change that may imply, at least at the beginning of the process, more chaos. The manipulation of history by Putin's regime is convincingly described by the British historian Jade McGlynn, a researcher in the War Studies department at King's College London, in her 2023 book *Memory Makers: The Politics of the Past in Putin's Russia*. In a country where the government has rendered its view of history and political events as the only possible and legitimate opinion, everyone's view of history has been turned into a security risk. In emphasizing cultural and spiritual values and historical truth, Putin aims to persuade Russian citizens that Russia needs a strong state, has a unique historical development, and above all is a great power that has much to offer the world. The tsarist era's identification of Moscow as the "Third Rome" after the Roman and Byzantine Empires seems to have returned with a vengeance. It was already present in Soviet times, as the Soviet Union's self-image was that of an actor at the center of the communist movement. According to McGlynn: "Through the Kremlin's actions, the suffering and heroism of the Soviet and Russian nations no longer belongs to them but to a government that distorts that experience for political ends and limits its citizens' freedom to learn about their traumatic and triumphant history."

It is true that the Russian language has two words for truth: *Istina* and *Pravda*. The first implies religious or spiritual truth, the second has connotations of justice. In Putin's rewriting of history there is the idea of a larger moral message that goes beyond factual truth. In Putin's time, like in Trump's time, truth is just "relative."

This absolute control over history was much less present at the very end of the Soviet regime, under Gorbachev, the only "human" leader – "too human" some would say – the Soviet Union ever had. I remember the long walk I had in the Gardens of Versailles with a very distinguished Soviet colleague in the late 1980s, before the fall of the Berlin Wall. We were alone and I was telling him how much I loved Russian culture but how much I loathed Russian political culture. He, maybe encouraged by my combination of empathy and criticism, wanted to open his heart to me. "You have to realize, to understand us, how much we have suffered in this twentieth century, and what will come to an end in a little more than a decade. No country in Europe has suffered more from the two world wars. But," he added, "the Soviet Union, through enforced famine and political executions, has killed more of its children than the foreign armies did. Even in quantitative terms, in comparative casualties, we have been our own worst enemy." His argument was strong and disturbing. Is this how Russia thanked its children for having fought so bravely in World War I and even more so in the Great Patriotic War?

At a time when disinformation, myths, and false narratives already reigned supreme, and when independent historians were still – though less aggressively – persecuted, it took some courage to overturn the very core of the official tale of the Soviet Union's admirable courage and triumphant results. Since the beginning of the war in Ukraine, the Russian regime has taken an even darker path, one from which any return seems a remote process as long as Putin remains in power. In the context of today's Russia, Putin may find the words to present defeat as victory. But there are limits to this process, even in the "empire of lies" that Russia has become. It is difficult not to think that, in spite of its nuclear arsenal, its oil and gas wealth, Putin's Russia in one way or another is doomed, as well as its leader himself. But when and how? "Besides raw material and political thuggery, the only things Russia exports are talented people . . . Putin styles himself as a new tsar. But a real tsar would not have to worry about a looming succession crisis and what it might do to his grip on power in the present," writes Stephen Kotkin, the great specialist on Russia ("Russia's divergent futures," *Foreign Affairs* May/June 2024). In fact, Russia can navigate through its own chaos, as long as the West weakens too. In terms of comparative decay, Russia seems unparalleled among great powers.

North Korea does not deserve a full treatment here – it is an outlier, whose destiny is to disappear and to merge with the very successful entity that South Korea has become over the course of the years; but there is another member of the Global East that does deserve consideration: Iran. And this for a combination of opposing reasons. It is a country at the threshold of becoming a nuclear power, but above all it may be a civilization that, in spite of the barbaric nature of its present rulers, is the inheritor of a great empire, the Persian Empire.

Religious despotism: the case of Iran

Iran is further proof that geography does not dictate the reordering of the world. Geographically, Iran may be in the Middle East, but from a geopolitical standpoint, the country, given its total opposition to the Western world, belongs without hesitation to the Global East. There exists a strange parallel between Iran and Israel. Two of the three non-Arab countries of the region (Turkey is the third) have in some ways moved out of it. Israel is part of the Western world, and Iran part of the Eastern one. Uncertain of their geographic identity, the two countries are simply obsessed with each other. Tehran draws its legitimacy in the Arab/Muslim world from its radicalism on the subject of Israel, a Zionist entity that has no right to exist as an independent state in the Middle East. In fact, in their respective evolutions, these two mortal adversaries act as if they were accomplices in a potentially suicidal game, each camp in its growing extremism justifying the hardening of the other. Of course, the differences are enormous between the two countries. Iran, a despotic regime, does not hesitate to shoot to kill to repress any dissidence within its regime. Israelis may shoot at Palestinians; they do not (so far at least) – with the tragic exception of the assassination of Prime Minister Rabin in 1995 – shoot their own citizens.

Who could have predicted nearly forty-five years ago that the religious fanatics who had just seized power would still control the country today? I remember a dinner at the Iranian Embassy in the mid-1980s, where caviar was served with Coca Cola, and the "sophisticated" prediction I shared with my wife upon my return: "A regime that mixes caviar with coke cannot survive for long." Today, the regime is not only still alive, it is more brutal than ever, and behaves in a harsher way than ever before. Holding a deep belief that the only way to fully control a society is through terror, the regime has drawn the dual lessons from the fall of the Shah in 1979, and the fall of Saddam Hussein in Iraq in 2003. To resist popular dissent, you should not hesitate to shoot your own people. Reza Pahlavi fled to Egypt without putting up a real fight; in China, protestors at Tiananmen Square were brutally suppressed in the spring of 1989; and, until recently, the Assad regime was firmly in control in Syria. Iran is certain that brutality, if not sheer terror, is its only chance of survival. Beyond the direct use of violence, there is the threat of using weapons of terror, including nuclear ones. Tehran is convinced that if Saddam Hussein had had at his disposal real and not imaginary weapons of mass destruction, the regime would still be in place, and the Americans would not have dared to invade Iraq to overthrow the regime. The reasoning in Pyongyang seems to be the same as in Tehran. Nuclear weapons are sought as an instrument of survival for the regime rather than as an instrument of deterrence for the country. This nuance is important, even if the two dimensions are inextricably linked. The case of Iran is of course much more sophisticated than the North Korean model. The Islamic Republic of Iran is a state divided against itself. Since the 1979 revolution, it has been defined by an existing tension between the president who heads its elected government, and the supreme leader who leads the parallel state institutions that embody modern Iran's revolutionary Islamist ideals. With the election of Ebrahim Raisi to the presidency in 2021 and the triumph of the hardliners, the parallel state seems to have won over the official state – an evolution that has increased the despair and the sense of despondency in what remained of civil society, especially in the big cities. As demonstrations multiplied in Iran, after the absurd murder of a young Iranian/Kurd woman, who had committed the inexcusable crime of not wearing her veil properly, I thought for a while that, this time, "it was different," and that the Persian Spring would succeed where the Arab Springs had failed. Terror has so far washed away those dreams, but for how long? There is something like a tight race between the growing collapse of the Iranian regime and its proximity to acquire nuclear weapons. Which will come first? If I were to follow my intuition, I would say that the most probable scenario is that of a nuclear Iran, without the Islamic Republic. Iran will eventually have the bomb, and will get rid of their clerics. The question is: in which order?

If the Global South is animated by resentment and the Global East by anger, what is the dominating emotion of the Global West? Could it be fear, combined with resilience in confronting external threats, and extreme internal polarization?

4

The Global West between Polarization and Resilience

What is the Global West?

It would be tempting to define the Global West as the ensemble of countries that share a common democratic ideal and are united behind an essentially status quo vision of the world: to put it bluntly, we might call them the rich and the satisfied. This would not only be a gross oversimplification, but in fact a complete misunderstanding of today's reality. The West may be united "on paper" by a common democratic ideal. Yet what characterizes above all the Global West today – with the significant exception of the Asian West (Japan, South Korea, Australia, New Zealand, Taiwan) – is that the biggest risk to the stability, security, and wellbeing of its members comes not from the outside, but from within itself. Russia is an objective and dangerous threat, China an aggressive rival, terrorism an ever-present and ever-growing menace, reinforced by the developments in the Israel/Palestine conflict since October 2023. Above all, on the two sides of the Atlantic, America and the European Union are united by what divides them from within: the rise of populism. They are united by a common rejection of their elites, a growing intolerance of the point of view of the "other," and a common fear of the "migrant others," whether they are coming from Central or Latin America in the case of the United States, or from Africa and the Middle East in the case of Europe. A country like the United States, a former "imperial republic" to quote the title of one of Raymond Aron's books, cannot stand tall in the long run, cannot be fully effective in the world, cannot be viewed as a reliable or predictable leader or partner, if it is so divided against itself, if there is no agreement on fundamentals among its citizens. In terms of internal division, countries such as the United States and Israel (and, indeed, Poland, which hopefully is overcoming some of its deepest divisions), or groups of countries, such as the European Union, are faced with a common and urgent challenge. In the worst-case scenario – very unlikely but not totally impossible – the United States could be confronting civil war, whereas the European Union would just face disintegration and the end of the beautiful project that evolved from dream to reality (and tomorrow to nightmare?) in the aftermath of World War II.

The countries in the Global West may therefore present themselves as a "Gentlemen's Club," united by shared democratic values, and common ideals and interests. A club that still looks very attractive, at least to outsiders, but its internal divisions are growing dangerously, to the point where they risk becoming unmanageable. A situation that in turn could lead to a major crisis in the Western model of democratic capitalism.

Hopefully, we are not there yet. And it would be dangerous to bury prematurely the Global West. But it is no longer enough to count on the survival instinct and ultimate rationality of its members, to declare that, in the end, everything will turn out to be all right, because, fundamentally, the vulnerabilities of the Global South and the Global East are deeper and more intractable than "ours."

The West is no longer the center of the world

To face what is above all a unique political and cultural identity crisis, the West has first of all to accept the fact that it is no longer the center of the world. The West also has to accept that the roots of its problems are ancient, and were widely known before the present explosion of polarization. Because they were not addressed sooner, much less confronted, these problems have become much more serious. One of the underlying reasons for this is a sort of political escapism. "I know what I should do for the wellbeing of my countrymen," a prominent politician from Luxembourg used to say, "but I do not know how to be re-elected if I were to do it." Some challenges seem to be intractable, such as the highly symbolic case of gun control in the United States, or the migration issue on both sides of the Atlantic, or societal issues such as abortion, same-sex marriage, and wider gender issues. These questions are simply too divisive, too emotional, to be confronted head-on. That is at least how most governments behave. But, to quote Simon and Garfunkel again, "silence like a cancer grows." "If I do not choose, that is still a choice," wrote Jean-Paul Sartre in his book *Existentialism Is a Humanism*. Unresolved problems are eating up the credibility, legitimacy, and workability of the democratic system, and of its representatives.

America's democratic challenges: from the land of hope and glory to the land of fear and worry

In the immediate aftermath of Barack Obama's election in 2008, the *International Herald Tribune* published a very moving cartoon summarizing the significance of the event. It depicted a white man and a black man in each other's arms. There were tears on the face of the black man. The entire world was watching, each continent represented by a distinct character, recognizable by their clothing. The blurb accompanying the cartoon said it all: "Yes, they could."

This positive vision of the United States – one of the high points of America's soft power – has given way, since the election of Donald Trump in 2016, and even more so since January 6, 2021, and the deliberate attempt to overthrow the results of the 2020 presidential election, to a strikingly different image of the United States in the world. One of dismay. In America, anger (if not rage) seems to have replaced the tears of reconciliation. For the country's original Enlightenment values are now faced with combined attacks stemming from the extreme right and the extreme left, from the populist ultra-nationalists to the Woke movement.

America is not alone in the Global West to be faced with these combined offensives, but one has nevertheless to start the tour of the Global West's inner challenges with the US, not necessarily because the problems there are in essence bigger (though that may very well be the case), but because the country, strategically, economically, culturally, and above all symbolically, is still, by a long way, the key pillar of the Global West (even after the triumphant victory of Donald Trump in November 2024). How can a country that is so deeply polarized – and one should not be afraid of using the expression "so much at war with itself" – be the incarnation of hope, legitimacy, and stability for the world? It is not only that it is difficult to preach to others what you no longer practice at home. In an international confrontation that has become ideological, living up to one's values matters even more. In a world where emotions and soft power (the two are closely linked) are becoming as important as hard power and cold Realpolitik calculus, the image America gives of itself affects not only its credibility, but its ability to play the global role that it is the only one capable of assuming in the Global West. The new war in the Middle East that started on October 7, 2023, has confirmed the ongoing unique role of the United

States but has also revealed its growing limits. Whatever its almost certain domestic political cost for Biden, Israel's darkest hour did reveal his finest moment. No one but the former President of the United States could have shown the same mixture of empathy for the victims, the same wisdom in telling Israelis not to fall prey to the spirit of revenge (in reference to America's past 9/11 mistakes in the region), and above all the same strength in deterring the Iranians – repeating three times to Tehran: "Don't, don't, don't." If deterrence works, we will never know of course what the Iranians' real intentions were.

But America's domestic weaknesses only serve to convince China, America's main rival, that the age of democracy is on the wane. Trump's re-election in November 2024 constitutes a confirmation, if not an ultimate encouragement, for Beijing and Moscow. They have both concluded that, even if they may be experiencing difficulties, the United States is in an even more dire situation than they are themselves.

The origins of polarization: from 9/11 to 1/6

Where does the present polarization in US politics come from? What are its roots? And, very concretely, is there a link (direct or indirect) between the fall of the Twin Towers in Manhattan on September 11, 2001 and the march on the Capitol on January 6, 2021?

Certainly, 9/11 was the product of an external threat. It was a tragedy that could only have a deep and lasting impact on the American psyche: the disturbing revelation of the country's vulnerability just when it was gloriously convinced of its superiority; after the fall of the Soviet Union, America was alone in its number one status. On 1/6, the attempt to seize the Capitol, the threat was domestic. The number of victims was small: five compared to the nearly three thousand killed during 9/11. But the impact of 1/6 may prove in the long run to be even more consequential. While 9/11 united Americans, 1/6 divided them. While 9/11 embodied the divorce between America and some significant parts of the world – in particular the Arab/Muslim world – 1/6 illustrated and aggravated America's domestic divorce. Nearly 50 percent of Americans still have doubts about the legitimate results of the 2020 presidential election. In the land of the *Federalist Papers*, the very fact that the notions of truth and justice may have been relativized by oppressive minorities who place any kind of tribal partisan solidarity above any sense of responsibility toward their country and its institutions is a traumatic turning point.

Ultimately, there is a link between 9/11 and 1/6, between the consequences of the war on terror and the consolidation of the extreme right in America. Caught by self-assured hubris at the peak of its power, America had underreacted in the mid- and late 1990s as it faced the rise of terrorist actions against. And, like a wounded animal, it overreacted after 9/11, launching itself into a series of unfortunate military adventures in the Middle East, and creating on its own territory a climate that favored the rise of extremism. In her 2020 book *Hate in the Homeland: The New Global Far Right*, Cynthia Miller-Idriss reaches the conclusion that the war on terror "supercharged" the far right. This phenomenon is clearly not limited to the United States, and is present in key European countries such as Great Britain and Germany, not to mention Italy, France, or even Sweden. In the wake of the 9/11 attacks, the rise of violent jihadism reshaped American politics in ways that created fertile grounds for right-wing extremism. "The attacks," writes Miller-Idriss, "were a gift to peddlers of xenophobia, white supremacism, and Christian nationalism: as dark-skinned Muslims, foreigners bent on murdering Americans . . . seemed to have stepped out of a far-right feverish dream." (The assassination of middle-school teachers, the first in 2020, and the second more recently in 2023, by Muslim terrorists in France, is, in the same vein, a gift for the extreme right.) But the aggression against American lives and values did not only come from the outside. It had its internal roots as well. The terrorist attack that took place in Oklahoma City in 1995 was, like other such attacks, the product of white supremacists, and it occurred six years before 9/11.

Economic insecurity: the fall of the Lehman Brothers "tower"

With hindsight, one is tempted to say that economic insecurity proved to be an even more fertile ground than physical insecurity for the growth of populism that led to the complete polarization of American society and politics. From that standpoint, the fall of the tower of Lehman Brothers Inc. on September 15, 2008, nearly seven years to the day after 9/11, proved to be a decisive turning point. Little more than a year later, in January 2009, I was the first holder of the Pierre Keller Visiting Chair of Government at Harvard University. Barack Obama had just moved into the White House. The weather, as is often the case in New England in the winter, was bitterly cold. I vividly remember seeing white people (mostly males) in their forties begging on Harvard Square, the very center of this small university town in Cambridge, Massachusetts. They had lost their jobs, some their homes too. I was shocked and worried by the contrast that existed between what I could hear on TV – Barack Obama's glorious and illuminating speeches – and what I could see in the streets. The pain, the misery, the humiliation. Given my French background, this plight made me think immediately of the French Revolution. To be fair, I had the same false intuition in France, forty years earlier in May 1968, thinking for a (very) few days that I was in 1789, and that the Revolution was around the corner.

In 2009 in the streets of Cambridge, I asked myself what I thought then to be very Western (universal?) questions. If nothing was done to alleviate the sufferings of such people, when would they reach the White House or the Capitol to express their fury, their anger? We now have the answer. It took them exactly twelve years. For on January 6, 2021, encouraged if not mobilized by an ex-president who would not recognize his defeat, "disgruntled" Americans, animated by deep anger if not hatred and a total absence of respect for the sanctity of American institutions, marched on the Capitol. In visual terms, the images coming live from Washington, DC looked like a modernized version of the "seizure of the Palace of the Tuileries," the Parisian residence of the king in August 1792. The Capitol building itself had been inspired by eighteenth-century European architecture, inspired in turn by Roman architecture. Of course, the differences between 1792 and 2021 were significant. In Washington, the demonstrators (should we say the "mob") were coming from the extreme right, not the extreme left. In some ways, one could describe them – this is certainly how they saw themselves – as ultra-legitimists. They wanted to reinstall, not overthrow, their defeated republican monarch. In sum, January 2021 was a mixture between an attempted coup and a revolutionary counterrevolution. In emotional, if not ideological, terms, it was also the indirect (direct?) product of the financial and economic crisis of 2007–9. In 2009, Barack Obama dedicated all possible government resources to salvaging the financial system. As a result, those who were at the root of the financial crisis were not punished, contrary to the innocent victims who were abandoned by a state that had practically no money left to come to their rescue. One of the vice-presidents of Lehman Brothers, whom I knew well, ended up teaching ethics at the University of Columbia in New York! He had lost money (a lot, even) but had kept his penthouse on Park Avenue.

America does not have a "welfare state" tradition, unlike the UK or France, but this time the feeling (and the reality) of pain was accompanied by a deep sense of injustice. The elites in Washington, as usual, had sacrificed the middle classes, left the "white trash" to their fate, condemned to live in their cars, their mobile homes, even the streets. And on top of it, at the helm, the president – to add insult to injury – was black, the first black president of the United States. The victims of the financial crisis were not only suffering, they were humiliated. I had naively thought that, with the election of Barack Obama, the wall of skin color had fallen for good in the United States, just as the wall of oppression had fallen on November 9, 1989 in Berlin. (Although, in recent years, we are witnessing in Germany, at least in the former Eastern part, a frightening rise of the extreme right – the AFD – not to mention the Neo-Nazis. It is as if, over eighty years, the vaccination against fascism has been slowly evaporating.)

In America, in reality, it was exactly the opposite: Obama was too black for the white middle class and, of course, for the white supremacists; and he was not black enough, and much too naturally aristocratic and distant, for a Black community that did not recognize him as one of them. Unlike his wife Michelle, he was not an Afro-American, i.e. a descendant of slaves. His father was a member of Africa's elites; his mother was white.

Confronted with a pile of unaddressed and therefore unsolved problems, from pure racism to violence, from decaying infrastructures that made citizens feel they were living in a third world country, to deeply divisive societal issues such as abortion, same-sex marriage, and gender choice, America was faced in the years that followed Obama's two terms of office with the worst political identity crisis of its relatively short two-century-old history, at least since the American Civil War (1861–5).

The particular responsibility of the Republican Party

Once again, as in the 1860s, Americans are divided on fundamentals. And they have to ask themselves questions such as: "What does it mean to be an American?" "What is the meaning of such key words as truth and justice?"

There is obviously an institutional dimension to America's problem. How can a constitution that was conceived for a small, emerging, and relatively homogeneous republic at the end of the eighteenth century still fit the needs of an internally diverse world power in the twenty-first century? Critics of America's institutions often make the point that the electoral college should be abolished. In a well-functioning democratic system, no one should be elected president with only a minority of votes in their favor, which was the case of Donald Trump in 2016. This complex, indirect system of voting has played in favor of the Republican Party over the past several decades and, currently, the party is deep in a structural and moral crisis, moving to the extremes step by step, and losing any sense of dignity and respect for its adversaries and, above all, for America's nearly sacred institutions. The Founding Fathers of the American Republic would be turning in their graves if they could see what has happened to the party of Abraham Lincoln, the GOP (the Grand Old Party). Shrewd and ambitious manipulators such as Donald Trump have simply taken full control of the party with the help of an aggressive minority, on the one hand, and the apathy, if not absolute cowardice, of political figures, on the other, who, with very few exceptions, have demonstrated an absence of dignity beyond belief. Henry Kissinger himself "played" with Donald Trump in his desire to remain close to power. But at what price? Watching the evolution of American politics, it is difficult not to think of Philip Roth's novel, published in 2004 – *The Plot Against America* – turned into a very powerful mini-series in 2020. The extremist temptation can even lead to a rewriting of history. During the first Trump administration, I had a dinner in Paris with an American billionaire, a Harvard graduate from Texas. He was deeply religious and sophisticated and obviously disturbed by Trump's personality. But, as he told me very directly, "Trump is the only one able to get the job done." For my interlocutor, the entire course of American history had to be revisited and redressed. In his eyes, America's participation in World War I and World War II were terrible and useless mistakes. His father had landed on the beaches of Normandy on June 6, 1944, and, following the bloodbath, he had quickly been promoted to captain. My dinner companion was not proud of his father, and certainly felt no empathy toward a person like me, who owed his life to the fact that his father had been liberated from a concentration camp by American GIs on May 8, 1945. Apart from his considerable wealth, this man was no exception in the new Republican Party. He represented, to the point of being a caricature of, the "America First," the "America Alone" stance of the Trump administration. *Foreign Policy Begins at Home* is the title of a short and powerful book, published in 2013, by the then president of the American Council on Foreign Relations in New York, Richard Haass; his subtitle is "The Case for Putting America's House in Order." For Haass, internal reforms, such as taking care of infrastructure problems, were part of the foreign policy message of the United States. You cannot be great outside, if you are weak, or perceived as such, inside.

Trump and his accomplices constituted then, and do so even more since his re-election, the greatest threat to the soft power of the United States and to the legitimacy of the democratic cause in the world. Why should anyone die for a cause that is discredited by the words and the deeds of the president of the United States?

If one looks for culprits in this crisis of democracy in America, the Republican Party has played a major role, by allowing itself to be taken over by Trump and his MAGA (Make America Great Again) movement. A culminating moment in this trend took place in October 2023, with the ousting of the Republican speaker of the House by a very small group (eight) of radical Republicans, furious with him for the compromise he had managed to reach with the House Democrats to avoid yet another possible budget shutdown of the American government.

Republicans should have realized early on that populism and conservatism are not necessarily compatible. RINO (Republican in Name Only) is the expression that Trump likes to throw at rivals in his own party. In reality, it's the ex-president himself who has abandoned the conservative values of the GOP. As British-born historian and essayist Simon Schama says: "Donald Trump is the real RINO." Populists may describe themselves as conservatives, but what they mean by that is simply "far righter than thou." Schama argues that Steve Bannon, once a close advisor to President Trump, who fell from his good grace but nevertheless remains in the limelight, is "about as much a conservative as the National Socialists of the Third Reich were socialists." Classical conservatives in postwar America – men like Russell Kirk and William F. Buckley Jr., editor of the *National Review* – emphasized fiscal responsibility, limited government, and a forward-looking position in the world, based on American leadership. Such classic conservatives would have been dismayed by Trump's description of January 6 as "a beautiful day," given that it was one of the darkest days in American history. One that saw the attempted sabotage of the Constitution. Mainstream Republicans are so terrorized by the grassroots of their party that they are all – with a few notable exceptions, such as Mitt Romney, who has left politics, and Chris Christie, the former governor of New Jersey who was a candidate against Trump in the Republican primaries – ready to declare that black is white or vice versa, in order to exist in a party so thoroughly controlled by Donald J. Trump. Trump is perceived as the savior, in almost religious terms – a heresy given that he is so totally agnostic – yet he is happy to take on the mantle of the martyr for the sake of all the "regular folks suffering from the condescension of liberals."

The problem with the Republican Party is that its primary mission should have been to protect the American Constitution from Trump and all those who identify as MAGA

supporters. They should have been revulsed by what happened on January 6, when, as Liz Cheney, daughter of Dick
Cheney, vice-president under George W. Bush, put it: "Donald
Trump summoned the mob, assembled the mob and lit the
flame." Even such an arch-conservative as John Bolton, who
briefly served as Trump's National Security Advisor, came to
understand that the ostensible leader of the free world was
himself the clearest and possibly most present danger to the
survival of the freedoms that America is supposed to stand for.
The absolute authority of the Constitution and the sanctity
of the truth ought to be the primary concerns of Republicans
and Democrats alike. If one were to follow the injunctions
of Section 3 of the 14th Amendment, Trump, who engaged
in insurrection, should have been disqualified from running
for re-election. The measure was originally intended after the
Civil War to deny ex-Confederates a path back into public
office. Of course, Trump, regardless of his acts and unlike the
Confederates during the Civil War, is not responsible for the
death of 600,000 Americans. The problem is more political
than judicial. Would disqualifying him from running have
been taking too great a risk, one that could have led to severe
clashes between his fanatical followers within the Republican
Party and all those who, like the author of these lines, consider
Trump to be the biggest danger that has ever existed in the
history of the American Republic? The first President of the
United States, George Washington, thought that it was essential for the effective functioning of government that "public
opinion be enlightened." The opposite process is at work
today, in a world dominated by systemic disinformation and
the multiplication of fake news. Can America recover from
structural racism, exploding inequality, economic crisis, and
democratic recession? "Restoring American leadership must
include the basic task of showing that the United States is a
capable problem solver once more," wrote Samantha Power, a
former ambassador to the United Nations in Barack Obama's

second term from 2013 to 2017. In other words, to defeat populism you have to show you can make a difference for the better in the lives of Americans. But is this enough? Joe Biden made a difference for the better in so many sectors, including the economy. But this was not sufficient for Kamala Harris on election day. In the immediate aftermath of Joe Biden's daring trip to Israel in October 2023, following the terrorist attacks by Hamas, public opinion polls in the US showed it to have had very little to no impact on his rating. In the UK, Churchill lost the election right after World War II. The war was over and the British wanted to turn over the page of glory and bravery, for one of welfare and comfort.

' In November 2024 in America, the *zeitgest* (the spirit of the time) led to the clear-cut victory of Donald Trump and the negative values for which he stands: fear of migrants, rejection of elites, the quest for a commander-in-chief (and certainly not a Black woman probably too satisfied with herself). Trump was not elected in spite of his excesses, brutality, and vulgarity, but because of them.

Woke is not left

In the same way that populism is not conservatism, so woke is not left, to paraphrase the title of a provocative book published in 2023 by the American philosopher Susan Neiman, *Left Is Not Woke*. I may be an old, arch-traditional, white, Western man, in love with the universal principles of the Enlightenment, but I refuse to see how the holders of this open and potentially generous philosophy can be accused of exclusively fostering capitalism and imperialism at the expense of the rest of the world. What I deeply feel is that, at a time when the planet is on fire, physically and metaphorically, the absolute obsession of the woke movement with identity politics seems not only out of touch with reality, but an individualistic obsession bordering on selfish narcissism. How can one spend so much time and energy on the issue of gender, very often one's own gender, when migrants are dying by the thousands in the Mediterranean or on their way to the Rio Grande in their attempt to simply survive? Such self-centered obsession with past pain can only create more pain. Without justice, peace and reconciliation are impossible in the long run, but an absolute conception of justice constitutes an obstacle to progress. Woke: the name was popularized by the fight against racism of the Black Lives Matter movement. "Wake up," for a man of my generation, is redolent of the leftists of May 1968. I could not follow them then, and I cannot follow their heirs now. Like the leftists of May 1968, they will probably become marginalized in the course of time through their excesses, their virulence. Of course, it is because of their excesses that they exist at all. They constituted such a useful punching ball for candidates to the leadership of the Republican Party, such as Florida governor Ron DeSantis. But am I totally wrong in thinking they are part of a cycle that will not remain for long in a position that could be described as the exact opposite of kingmaker: king-destroyer? Yet the woke movement harmed the presidential chances of a moderate Democratic candidate, as the US electorate, moved by passion, decided it could not choose between two evils and, instead, opted for a dangerous abstention. The war in Gaza has certainly reinforced the frustrations of the left wing of the Democratic Party toward Joe Biden, who is perceived as too favorable toward Israel. But in the end, it did not play a decisive role in the results of the 2024 elections.

The crisis of the European West

Internal polarization is not just an American problem. It also concerns the other key members of the Global West, above all the European Union and its member states, including the UK, which voted to leave the EU in 2016.

Mind you, there are some Europeans who wish the worst for America in the hope that an accelerated evolution of the United States toward anarchy and chaos will give the rest of the Western world, Europe first and foremost, the legitimacy to build its own strategic autonomous project. Is the eventual collapse of the United States the golden opportunity that Europe has been waiting for, to finally exist as a mature adult? Europeans behaved for far too long like adolescents oscillating between the urge to rebel and take their independence and the need to be protected by an America that, in spite of its young age (in comparative terms with Europe), had become a father figure.

But is Europe doing so much better than the United States that it can justify such a new status?

From war in Ukraine to war in the Middle East

The war in Ukraine constituted a major test for Europe, a test that it has (initially at least) passed with success, in spite of the selfish tendency of most European leaders and the populist calculus of a few others (first and foremost Victor Orbán in Hungary). But the return of war in Europe, beyond the legitimate emotion it has created, raises a longer-term question that is of an existential nature. Can Europe ever become a geopolitical actor when it has such difficulty developing a common position on its three major challenges? The issues of migration, climate change, and AI: to which one should probably add the issue of fanaticism of all brands, from Islamic fundamentalism to the fanatics of national sovereignty. One has also to add to these concerns – and they are closely linked – the return with a vengeance of the Middle East conflict. The fifth Israeli war, which started on October 7, 2023 (after the war of independence in 1948, the Suez Canal war in 1956, the Six-Day war in 1967, and the Kippur war in 1973) has revealed the depth of the emotional confusion that exists in Europe. Namely, how to show solidarity with Israel as it is confronted on its territory by sheer barbarism, while demonstrating its support for the Palestinian cause and that country's right to be recognized as an independent state alongside Israel? Europeans should have been able to demonstrate unity and moral clarity by declaring without ambiguity that there are degrees of evil: Israel's "sin of occupation" not being at the same level as the decapitation of children, the rape and slaughtering of women, the taking of hostages among the elderly and the very young. Unfortunately, there was no such cohesion. When the President of the European Commission went to Israel to express sympathy for the beleaguered Israeli population, criticisms immediately escalated. "You did not consult us, you have not denounced in the same vein the Israeli bombings of Gaza." It is interesting to note that the Germans (the President of the Commission is German, and reacts as such) are generally criticized when they make the right moral choice: in 2015 when they opened their doors to a million plus migrants, and in 2023 when they opened their heart to Israel. Germany now has a large Muslim population, but the weight of the past and its special relationship with Israel, a direct product of their repentance for the Nazi years, take priority over any other consideration. That is not the case in France, for example, where President Macron tries, not always with success, to maintain a balance between the two protagonists of the conflict. There was a time when Israeli diplomats were openly wishing that the German position would not be dissolved in any kind of "European" vision, much less favorable to the Jewish state.

Europe is in large part responsible for what is happening today in the Middle East. In 2000, the Palestinian intellectual Sari Nusseibeh and I were honored in Brussels at the seat of the European Parliament for writing on the Middle East with "moderation" and concern for the point of view of the "other." We both had to deliver a short speech. Sari chose to recall the history told to him by his mother as a way of summarizing the origins of the conflict in the metaphorical terms I mentioned earlier in the Introduction – it is Europeans, in effect, who were pushing Jews out of a window onto the heads of Palestinians below. One may or may not accept this Palestinian version of the story. In any case, the metaphor rightly points to the culpability of Europe.

As time went by, the images of October 7 were progressively replaced by much more numerous images of the civilian victims of Gaza. Failing to take into account the warning President Biden gave them – "Do not repeat our post-9/11 mistakes" – Israel's prime minister has contributed significantly to accelerating the natural process of time, and the shift from one emotion to another. On May 28, 2024, when the Republic of Ireland, along with Norway and Spain, recognized Palestine as an independent state, the Palestinian flag was raised alongside those of Europe and Ukraine in front of the Irish Parliament. This was a highly symbolic and emotional image that seemed to complete Israelis' journey, in the Irish imagination, from being fellow anti-imperialists fighting for independence from Britain in the 1930s to being colonizers in a new Northern Ireland, with the British now perceived not as unjust opponents of Zionism but of having forced Jews and their alien religion on the Palestinian natives. Empathy for Palestinians has replaced guilty feelings toward Jews, especially among young Europeans (and for that matter Americans), whose knowledge of history is too often minimal. In the eyes and the hearts of the Western world too, Israel has largely self-isolated itself. Can the continent that has been led to the abyss by the antisemitism of some be the originator of a peace solution in the Middle East? For this to happen, Europe would have first to be united. And, second, it would need to have the means and the will to exert influence on Israel, to save the Jewish state from itself. At the moment, Europe and the United States are simply not "boxing" in the same category. To believe that Paris and Berlin could use their experience in reconciliation to serve Israelis and Palestinians is a noble, generous, and visionary hope, but unfortunately it is unrealistic. Europe's priority is to protect itself from the risks of proliferation of the Middle East conflict into their territory; it is not to bring about peace there.

Can Europe ever become a geopolitical actor?

To understand Europe's dilemma, one has to go back at least to the very beginning of the twenty-first century. Robert Cooper, a talented and creative British diplomat working for the EU, had just published a short and provocative book, *The Post-Modern State and the World Order.* Europe, precisely because it neither pretended to be nor could become a geopolitical actor in the classical sense of the term, was not only modern, but was opening the path to the future. Europe was quintessentially a postmodern actor in a postmodern world. In fact, it was "the" model for all others to follow. A stable and prosperous economy, a Gentlemen's Club, which was about to extend membership to the center and the east of the continent, after having expanded in the south. Precisely because Europe was a unidimensional power and not a global one (which would have bogged it down with costly and largely useless military expenditures) it was, in its own (mostly German?) way the "shining light on the hill" on this side of the Atlantic. Of course, more skeptical minds – such as the author of these lines – wondered whether Europe could ever really be a model without being a full-fledged multidimensional actor. How can you press for the implementation or respect of values and principles you believe in if you lack the minimal elements of hard power, and, even more so, the will to take risks? As early as 2003, Europe's divisions over the second Gulf War were a sign of deep vulnerability, even if those who abstained from supporting the war effort were proven right by history. How can you be an actor if you disagree on fundamentals, and if your disagreements are exposed and denounced by your main ally, the United

States? But more perhaps than the division – to quote Donald Rumsfeld, who was then the defense minister under Georges W. Bush – between New Europe (those countries in Central and Eastern Europe, as well as the UK and Denmark, that supported Washington) and Old Europe (those that opposed the war, such as France and Germany), it is the passive unity post-2008 that has exposed the European Union's geopolitical weakness. In his largely autobiographical book, *Homelands: A Personal History of Europe*, the British historian and essayist, Timothy Garton Ash, described the year 2008 as marking the beginning of a pause in what had been a thirty-five-year story of the enlargement of the geopolitical West, not so much because of Russian pushback, but mainly because of "enlargement fatigue."

Fear of Putin (temporarily?) united Europeans behind Ukraine in 2022–3. But the consequences of a long and deep culture of "geopolitical irresponsibility" have limited the extent of Europe's help. The members of the Union simply do not have the military resources, equipment, or ammunition at their disposal to fill the mounting needs of the Ukrainian army. If Europe wants to stand up to the return of Geopolitics, with a capital "G," it must attain a sufficient degree of unity, central authority, and effective decision-making to defend its shared interests and values. To make a long story short, the EU must give up the veto power that each of its members has. Otherwise, it will falter, internally and externally. Can this be achieved? Will it prove any easier to adopt the majority vote within the EU than to enlarge the composition of the permanent members of the UN Security Council? The answer is far from obvious. The smaller you are within the EU, the more attached to your veto power you tend to be. And you do not have to be small to be "supercharged" with nationalism. The example of Poland under the direction of Law and Justice (PiS) is a case in point. One of the best pieces of news of late (maybe the only really good one) has been the defeat of the nationalist arch-conservatives in the October 2023 elections in Poland. Afraid of a divorce of values between them and Europe, a slight majority of Poles chose the voice of moderation, respect for democratic principles incarnated by the opposition led by Donald Tusk, a former prime minister and a former President of the European Council. By so doing, Poles have sent a message to Europe and the United States, if not the world: populism is not irresistible; the rise of illiberal democracy is not inevitable. Yet the political situation in Poland remains fragile and the PiS could return to power.

The very emotional marriage of reason between France and Germany

Each European country has its own history and culture and is dominated by its very own specific emotions. France and Germany, which still constitute the core of the EU, whose "marriage of reason" guaranteed the efficient functioning of Europe, are deep down divided by what unites them: a common obsession with their respective pasts. For Germany, Europe has been the ultimate protection against the return of the most infamous era of their past: the Nazi period. Postwar Europe has always been, on that front, the ultimate life insurance. It was worthwhile sacrificing what the Germans were most proud of, the Deutsche Mark, for the sake of making sure the past would never return.

The French too are obsessed with their past, but in their eyes it is essentially a past of greatness and glory. And all too often, "nothing fails more than success." For a very long time, some would tend to say until today, the French saw Europe as the mechanism that would allow their president to be the heir of the Sun King (Louis XIV) and Napoleon, to lead a great power through other means. This tendency to treat Europe as France-writ-large could be seen as a form of revenge over a history of recent defeats, but this time a symbolic revenge of a positive and enlightened nature. Embracing and attempting to lead Europe was just the opposite of what France did after being defeated in the Franco-Prussian war, when it turned to colonial adventures as a substitute for European power. Imperial enlargement in faraway territories then was replaced with a process of reconciliation and integration with France's biggest and most problematic neighbor. Yet Paris was still clinging to its obsession with balancing Berlin within the Union through a refined balance of unbalances. Germany was more prosperous, more dynamic economically, and, especially after reunification, more populated. France however, had very powerful counterweights: the nuclear bomb, a seat as a permanent member of the Security Council, and its tradition of military intervention in the world. Some of these "ingredients" could, of course, easily backfire and proved to be vulnerabilities – in particular, of late, France's interventionist tradition in Africa. Prisoner of their African past, the French have failed to perceive the depth of change and the globalization in that continent, where Germany and Turkey, and even more so China, have overtaken them as important trade and economic actors. When the French denounce, rightly, the new Russian imperialism in Africa, Africans answered them back: "Given your past, you are the least qualified persons to warn us about the dangers of imperialism."

Today, France and Germany seem united by a common sense of depression, a common lack of confidence in themselves. By dissolving, unnecessarily and irresponsibly, the National Assembly in June 2024 after poor results in the elections for the European Parliament, President Macron added confusion to disillusion. And the extreme right seems closer to power than it ever was in the history of the Fifth Republic.

The post-Brexit emotions of the United Kingdom

As for the other "big" European nation, the UK, it voted to leave the EU in 2016, pushed by populist leaders who exploited negative emotions, including fear about Europe's unfolding migrant crisis, and deliberately lied about the benefits of leaving the Union. As time goes by, slowly but surely, pragmatism and reason are coming back. The emphasis is no longer on cutting links in the most demonstrative way. The declared ambition of transforming the UK into a "Singapore on the Thames," so out of touch with reality, is no longer being used. What prevails is the subdued return of "John Bull" (a more pragmatic and mercantile version of the majority who said "Yes" to Brexit in June 2016). It can be said that, having gone beyond this explosion of irrationality in 2016, the UK has returned to become a model of pragmatism. The parliamentary elections in July 2024 opposed center-right and center-left forces. Extreme parties were largely absent, unlike in the countries of the rest of Europe. Should a moment of folly be the condition for the return of rationality? The UK will not return to the EU: nobody in Europe would want it back. But it is likely that London will try to progressively move closer to Brussels, taking small policy steps, maybe reaching the status of Norway and returning to be a member of the Common Market.

For the moment, compared to France and even Germany, the UK, under the discreet leadership of Keir Starmer, might almost resemble a model of rationality.

The singular case of Poland

The case of Poland is particularly interesting, an illustration of the contradictions that beset countries led by populist leaders. Since the beginning of the war in Ukraine, Poland has taken on a bigger role in Europe. Warsaw's plan is to build up the biggest army inside the EU (second, of course, to Ukraine, for a victorious Ukraine would have the largest and most combat-hardened armed forces in Europe outside of Russia). In other words, to become on the eastern front of NATO what Turkey is on its southern front. Poland has taken into its territory as many as 8 million Ukrainians, many of whom have returned to their homeland in spite of the continuation of the war. But that very Poland, active, open, and generous, is also the country that decided on the eve of its legislative elections to suspend the delivery of arms to Ukraine to attract the votes of its rural electorate, which wished to stand up to Kiev on the issue of cereal prices. To give priority to pure electoral considerations at this particularly important juncture was to risk sending the wrong signal to Moscow and its supporters, which would con-clude: "When we were telling you that the coalition formed to back Ukraine was fragile and would not last long, we were right."

There is another topic that constituted a source of concern and demonstrated the difficulty of the populist majority in Poland to concentrate on important questions. In a deliber-ate confusion of priorities, the Polish government escalated its anti-German rhetoric, even after the beginning of the war in Ukraine. The issue of reparations, for crimes committed by Nazi Germany eighty years ago during World War II, remains today a painful scar. But was this the right moment for such demands? Is the astronomical amount of the repara-tions demanded ($850 billion) a just one, whatever that means, given also the fact that Germany already paid reparations to Communist Poland? Fortunately, on October 15, 2023, the Poles voted this revanchist, ultra-nationalist majority out. But such grudges can still hang like a sword of Damocles over many a European election.

Toward a new enlarged Europe

Thanks to Putin, "enlargement fatigue" has given way (for how long?) to "enlargement necessity and inevitability." With the exception of Croatia, which slipped into the EU in 2013, the rest of the Western Balkans are still waiting at Europe's door, despite Brussels' promises. But now, with the acceptance in principle of Ukraine and Moldova as candidates, and an encouraging signal sent to Georgia, the situation has changed radically. The European Union in the foreseeable future might well turn into a club of thirty-plus countries (between thirty-six and forty if one adds all the potential candidates). In spite of its many shortcomings, Europe is slowly becoming a "hope of last resort." In an increasingly post-Western world, can one speak of an inevitable process of consolidation, based as much on fear as on hope? In a positive scenario, the future ahead of us will see a strengthening and an enlarging of the European West in geopolitical terms inside Europe, in an accelerating post-Western world. Is there an alternative scenario?

To make any sense, such enlargement requires a transformation of the EU. When the issue was first raised, there were two schools of thought. First, those who maintained, like France, that strengthening the union was a precondition for enlargement (and hoped that such "deepening," to use EU language, would make Turkey's accession impossible). And, on the opposite side, the British (that was at least the French interpretation), who wanted enlargement so as to make deepening impossible. I remember a conversation I had on the topic with President Nicolas Sarkozy. He wanted to know why I was favorable toward Turkey's candidacy. I told him that, for me, the road was more important than the result. As long as Turkey was a candidate for our club, it would be a better Turkey; the moment we say "No," the pull of the East would become irresistible. Sarkozy's answer was crystal clear: "Your position is much too sophisticated. The only thing I know is that 75 percent of French people are against the entrance of Turkey into the Union."

The Turkish economy may be much stronger than that of countries such as Bulgaria or Romania, but for the opponents of its candidacy, Turkey is not physically in Europe, except for a tiny part – and, of course, Turkey is Muslim.

Today, the key issue remains the same, except that the stakes have become even higher. Without "qualified majority voting," how could a club of thirty-plus function when, with twenty-seven members, it is already too often paralyzed? According to German Chancellor Olaf Scholz, qualified majority voting presupposes the consent of 55 percent of the member states, representing at least 65 percent of the bloc's population. It would be the best way to marginalize a representative of illiberal democracy, such as Victor Orbán's Hungary. Critics of the reform insist that it would also provide cannon fodder for unhappy populist leaders and extreme right-wing political parties. But what is easier to denounce: a weak Europe, paralyzed by its unanimity mechanisms, or a much stronger and more efficient Europe that becomes "a doer"? It is not so much a question of efficiency as a question of identity. Who will ultimately take a decision that can lead to war and the sending of European troops, against the will of some "minority" members of the Union? You can die for your country, but can you die for a group of nations that have deliberately failed to create a common emotion, beyond common interests and common values? Russia's motivations for fighting in Ukraine may be far weaker than Ukrainians' motivations in resisting, but what about European emotions? What makes a nation is a combination of clear boundaries and a clear historical and political narrative. And Europe so far has neither of these. Europe's boundaries are still fluctuating, and may continue to do so for a long time. As for its narrative, there may be something like an embarrassment of riches. The failure to write a common European textbook on the history of the continent that would be accepted and studied by all is highly symbolic of the difficulty to create a common European future. Without a commonly agreed past, how can we plan for a common future? Europe's message is losing on two crucial counts: it remains too paternalistic and arrogant toward the Global South and too uncertain and hesitant toward its own past and its future identity. How can we be credible in our universalist message while remaining so jealous of our national differences, and so incapable of transcending them with a complete reshuffling of our institutional framework?

The war in Ukraine has, at least initially, had one positive effect on Europeans, who have discovered their anti-Russian resilience. But it has also exposed the possible long-term depths of their diverging interests and emotional divides. Within the Union, there are more than nuances between those whose emotions are clearly pro-Israel, such as Ursula von der Leyen, and those who, like Josep Borrell, seem to feel more for the suffering of the Palestinian people than they do for the Israelis. On such topics, one is walking on eggs. It is a question of emphasis and nuances, and no one will willingly admit his or her priorities. But if all Europeans do not "feel the same" how can they speak and act together?

It would be tempting to say that, beyond the clashes between radicals and moderates, nostalgia for the past, or advocating progress – distinctions that correspond more to the reality of the present than the classical division between left and right – the largest party in Europe is the party of indifference. On subjects ranging from the migrants that have transformed the Mediterranean Sea into a huge cemetery to the roads of the Caucasus, where Armenian refugees felt they had no other choice but to flee for their lives and abandon their towns, their churches, and their homes, what dominates is passivity. A passivity that amounts to indifference. The fate of Armenia in 2023 is a case in point.

The two issues cannot be compared of course. What motivates European attitudes toward the migrants coming mostly from Africa and the Middle East is a combination of fear and rejection, reinforced after every terrorist attack on European soil, to the extent that implicit in many a European citizen's worldview is something like this: "My life is already sufficiently difficult as it is. Why should I add their problems to mine? All the more so because, in reality they will make my problems even more difficult to solve. They were born in the wrong place at the wrong time. It is their fate, not mine." The case of the refugees of Nagorno-Karabakh is of another nature. They have a place to go to: Armenia. But their fate has been decided by two powers, one Muslim, Turkey, one Christian, Russia, which were clearly not motivated by a sense of balance or justice. Might is increasingly prevailing over right, given the very complex nature of a territory that has changed hands so many times over the course of history. What remains are the images of thousands of refugees "on the road again." And also the lack of Western interest, as if the war in Ukraine had monopolized and in fact exhausted the possibility for empathy within the Western world for other distant Christian European cousins. More than twenty years ago, NATO intervened in the Balkans, in reaction to the spectacle of refugees forced into trains. In 2023, nothing of the kind occurred. Could it be that, though they are Christians from the Caucasus, Armenians are not perceived as Europeans? Like Georgians in 2008, they had hoped the West could come to their rescue. They were wrong. And their fate is a warning, if not a wake-up call, for all those who look to the European Union as their ultimate savior. As long as Europe is not a power, it can neither be a model nor a solution; it can only remain as a semi-functional bureaucratic dream.

Could Europe be prisoner of the past glory of some, and the past infamy of others, and the various complexes of so many who, like Hungary, are trying to turn into weapons what they perceived as the unfair treatment they were submitted to in the past? Victor Orbán, in this light, is the direct product of the Trianon Treaty that amputated nearly two-thirds of the territories that Hungary controlled before World War I.

Still too much of an empire in terms of its arrogant stance toward the Global South, Europe, in claiming to be a "legal empire" or a normative power, is not credible enough for the other powers in the world, be they China, Russia, or, perhaps more important, the United States. The isolationist right that wants Europe to take responsibility for their own continent – like Florida's governor, Ron DeSantis – have a point, which Europeans cannot continue to ignore for ever.

The Asian West

In contrast to a majority of the members of the Global South, Asian countries such as Japan or South Korea are not united by resentment against the West. Maybe this is because they feel more confident about themselves. But mostly because their humiliation did not come from the West, but from the East – China for some, Japan for others. And they are above all united now by a common and justified fear of China. Will such a shared fear enable Seoul and Tokyo to enter into a full spirit of reconciliation, allowing them to close the tragic pages of the past, when Japan occupied Korea, when Korean women were forced to serve as prostitutes for the Japanese army? There is nothing inevitable in such a reconciliation. The differences between the Franco-German reconciliation and a potential South Korean-Japanese one, are manifold. The French and the Germans both belonged to Europe and felt European in cultural terms. Do Koreans and Japanese feel Asian, a concept largely created and imposed on them by the West? For some analysts, like the Dutch writer and journalist Ian Buruma, repentance, a key step toward reconciliation, is a Christian concept totally foreign to the Japanese, who also have difficulties in integrating the needs and views of any "other" in their self-perception as an "absolute island." Nor should one forget the nuclear factor. After Hiroshima and Nagasaki, many Japanese felt they had more than paid for their crimes, that their atonement was complete. They were, furthermore, convinced that the West would not have used "the absolute weapon" against them if they had been white and Christian. After returning from a visit to the museum of the city of Hiroshima, which describes in every detail what happened to the city on August 6, 1945, and what happened to the survivors after, I was surprised that there was no explanation for what led to the use of the bomb on the city. August 6 was presented as an event coming from nowhere. Upon my return to Tokyo, I conveyed my surprise to a former Japanese ambassador to the United States. His answer – though not representative of the majority of the Japanese establishment – was nevertheless very interesting: "What is there to explain? The facts are so enormous and explicit in themselves." And he ended his remarks with a short and disturbing comment: "We will apologize to the Chinese and the Koreans, when Americans apologize for Hiroshima and Nagasaki!"

In Seoul, too, the past does not pass easily. I remember my first trip to South Korea in 1984. I was given a tour of Seoul by a former student of mine at the Paris Institute of Political Studies (Sciences Po). This visit was very politically oriented, and centered on the atrocities and urban destruction committed by the Japanese during their occupation period. It was more than forty years ago, and clearly today negative emotions are less violent than they used to be. But they are still there, as if the two parties were still unwilling or incapable of moving on the road toward reconciliation, in spite of the ever-stronger incentive that the Chinese threat represents. Confronted with the calculated madness of the North Korean regime and the rising nationalism, if not adventurism, of the Chinese in the South China Sea, the two countries should set aside the scars of the past and move toward a positive accommodation between two nations that have so many interests in common, that share the same democratic ideals and that possess a "soft power" that has grown exponentially in recent years. Both, in their respective traditions, remain decidedly "Asian," whatever that may mean, but Asian in a way that appeals to and influences the West the way their ancestors (the Japanese in particular) did at the end of the nineteenth century for example, when French Impressionists such as Claude Monet were greatly influenced by Japanese art.

The Asian West's security interests are largely identical to those of the West (nothing unites more than a common threat) and their sensitivities, if not emotions – product of the process of globalization of culture, from arts, televised series, and sports, without forgetting fashion – are increasingly in tune with each other.

There is another dimension that, in the Japanese and South Korean cases, makes the Asian West not so much a model as a warning. And that is of course the demographic situation, which is judged in Tokyo to be no longer serious, but quite simply catastrophic. In January 2023, Prime Minister Fumio Kishida did not mince his words. As he put it: "Japan is standing on the brink of an abyss as to whether we can continue to function as a society." The birth/death balance in the country means that its indigenous population is now shrinking at a rate of around one person every minute.

This sense of an unstoppable slow-motion disaster forced the Japanese, though they are very reluctant to admit it, or even discuss it openly, to introduce in 2019 a visa program that is, in effect, opening the country up to tens of thousands of blue-collar workers from overseas. Yet the core of the problem remains. Why is the unmarried population rising, and why are people marrying so late in life? Of course, the demographic situation of Japan may be seen as an advantage, since wages will increase as labor becomes scarce and housing sizes may expand. And the rise of wages might then encourage the Japanese to marry earlier and have children.

The concept of "Japanization," sometimes applied to China, refers to the economy and Japan's stagnant "lost decades" of the 1990s and 2000s. Could "Japanization" refer also to demographics and be applied to Europe's situation? From this standpoint, Italy, with its aging and shrinking population, is clearly being "Japanized." And my country, France, following Germany, is also moving in that direction. But the Asian West is only the avant-garde of a movement that is affecting the world at large (and not only the Western world), with falling fertility rates becoming one of the biggest challenges facing our world, moving from baby boom to baby bust.

Israel: the Middle Eastern West or the West in the Middle East

Just as Saudi Arabia or Egypt are undeniably key members of the Global South, and Iran in its aggressive stance is part of the Global East, so Israel belongs more than ever to the Global West because of its geopolitical situation, and also because of its internally polarized evolution. This association/ integration of Israel with the Global West is not as evident as it sounds. David Ben-Gurion, Israel's first prime minister, initially dreamed of the (re)nascent Jewish state as a bridge between the West and the South, particularly Africa. Looking at the present evolution of the Jewish state, one could easily be tempted to venture that Israel has of late been moving east, away from liberal democracy, toward illiberal democracy if not authoritarianism – even, to call a spade a spade, toward racism (in its most radical extreme right incarnation) – especially after october 7, 2023.

The founding fathers of the state of Israel were from Europe (more precisely, from the eastern part of the European continent). With the process of time and the growing role of the United States in the Middle East, Israelis who had contradictory feelings about their European Jewish roots – a continent they came from, but that had badly treated them through persecutions and pogroms, culminating with the Shoah – felt increasingly Western rather than European. For better or worse, their democratic status on the one hand, the polarization of their society leading to a near paralysis of their democratic system on the other, Israel is the illustration of the best and worst sides of the West. It is an illustration of the dangers of illiberal democracy, with Prime Minister "Bibi" (Benjamin Netanyahu) standing as a prefiguration of Trump. For decades, the West was an insurance of sorts, a model despite the heavy legacy of the past; a source of oxygen for a country that was mostly cut off from its region. But then a dual revolution took place. Israelis were able and eager to travel in a region that had finally (for how long?) opened its doors to them. The emotional and psychological weight of the Abraham Accords should not be underestimated. Culmination of the agreement would have been the full normalization of relations between Riyadh and Jerusalem. The region, which has a special responsibility over the three holiest places of Islam (Mecca, Medina, and Jerusalem's Al-Aqsa), was ready to open its arms, despite the unresolved (this is an understatement) fate of the Palestinians, to the state of Israel: an incredible transformation. Israelis felt for a short period of time that their legitimacy in the region could only increase exponentially thanks to the benediction of the Saudis (at least the green light of a daring de facto ruler, MBS).

This external supplement of legitimacy would have come precisely at the moment when the internal legitimacy deficit was taking on dangerous proportions. Never since the creation of the state of Israel in 1948 have Israelis been so divided on the essentials. In a sermon at the start of Yom Kippur (the Day of Atonement), the most sacred Jewish religious moment, the nationally prominent French liberal rabbi, Delphine Horvilleur, directly addressed the issue of polarization in Israel, reminding her audience that the Kingdom of Israel had ceased to exist twice because of divisions among the Jews – and on both occasions, this was after an existence of around seventy-five years. And now, the fatidic date (1948/2023) had returned. Were Israelis conscious of these terrible historical precedents? Going even further, the left-leaning Israeli newspaper *Haaretz* asked the question of whether the "Jewish people are capable of being a people with a country." The Israel/Palestine conflict used to be described as a "clash of calendars"; for Israelis, their independence as a state in 1948 was the late fruit of the nationalisms blossoming in late nineteenth-century Europe. For Palestinians, it was just an anachronism. The Jewish state was created in the Middle East just as the process of decolonization was gathering steam. In 2022/23, in the months leading up to October 7, another clash was coming to the fore, this time between Israelis. A clash between two conflicting projects and rationales. Why Israel? To create a safe place for the Jewish people, who had been victim of so many persecutions in particular in Europe? To build a democratic haven that would serve as a bridge between the West and the East? Or could it be to build a place where religious Jews would feel at ease, where the command of the Bible would come before any consideration for democratic process or the rule of law?

As a result of this clash of interpretations, of this fundamental disagreement on the nature of the Zionist project, today's Israelis, like Americans (at least up to October 7, 2023) seem to live in parallel realities. There is little that unites the ultra-liberal, sexually open, artistically, financially, and technologically modern, if not postmodern, "Tel-Aviv Republic," and the much more religious and conservative, if not ultra-conservative, "Kingdom of Jerusalem." Both use the Israeli flag in their respective demonstrations, both sing the national anthem, but it means utterly different things for them.

How can one summarize the divisions that have paralyzed (and continue to do so) the functioning of the state of Israel? For some actors and analysts, the clash of emotions that tears Israel apart opposes a theocratic vision of the state to a secular one. There is no need to search for further explanation. For others, this vision is far too simplistic and forgets the political debate between those who cherish the notion of a balance of power and respect for the rule of law. For these people (probably a majority), it is vital, especially for a state that does not have a written constitution, to preserve the independence of the Supreme Court as a guarantee that Israel will not fall prey to the diktat of those who occupy the reins of power and may be – even with a slim majority in the Knesset (the Israeli Parliament) – ready and willing to change the rules of the game.

These two Israels had (at least until October 7) little in common, except perhaps a common indifference to the plight of the Palestinians. A bit like the very poor in India or Brazil, Palestinians had become invisible. The expression is of course paradoxical for a population that is separated from the rest of the country by high walls. But obsessed with themselves and the prospect of a nuclear Iran, Israelis had no time to spend on a problem that seemed to have no solution.

Somewhere though, they must know that the present status quo is untenable. The two-state solution has long been abandoned (though not rhetorically). One pays regular tribute to it. It pleases the international community, and does not cost much. "If you set aside ambiguity it is always to your own detriment," the seventeenth-century French Cardinal de Retz used to say. Why not let the formula float? The other alternative, the one-state solution, has simply become impossible, unless it means the expulsion of all Palestinians (or all Israelis of course!). Israelis will not help Palestinians move in the direction of a two-state solution. Palestinians themselves seem to be convinced deep down that time (and demography) play in their favor. The stone of the land weighs more heavily than the Towers of Tel-Aviv. And if Israel had full control over the Palestinians in the "territories," could it then treat them openly as second-class citizens, no longer having to counter accusations of apartheid? The balance of forces between Israelis and Palestinians has become more unequal than ever (at least that was the perception that existed before October 7). "We know Hamas more than they know themselves," was a formula I heard more than once in the mouths of Israeli security officials. Abandoned by their "Arab Brothers" (at least by the regimes who rule them), betrayed if not abandoned by their unrepresentative and too often corrupt leaders, Palestinians had either chosen physically to leave a hopeless situation, or were retreating into anger, resentment, and despair, leading in a recurrent manner to explosions of violence. Over the past seven decades and more, Israelis have demonstrated their resilience; today, they give the impression of being on the verge of a nervous breakdown. From that standpoint, they are more than ever in the West, but as an exacerbated prefiguration of what can happen to Western democracies if they do not stop on their way to the abyss.

Since October 7, Israelis have been confronted with a maelstrom of emotions. One would be tempted to say that all the emotions mentioned in this book are present in Israel at one and the same time. There is fear, of course, after the worst pogrom the Jewish people have had to confront since the end of World War II – a pogrom that took place not in the distant lands of the east of Europe, but right in the center of the state that was created in 1948 to prevent the repeat of such catastrophes. The Jewish state was the last recourse, the ultimate life insurance, the supreme "Never Again." And yet, because of hubris on one side and absolute barbarism on the other, fear has returned at the very heart of Israeli and Jewish identity.

Beyond fear, there is humiliation, starting with the intelligence services and the army deemed to be "the best and the brightest" of the region. They were caught by surprise as "beginners" by a terrorist movement whose apparent "quietness" had made Israel, so to speak, "sleepy." Evil existed underground in a series of tunnels, whose existence was known, but whose efficiency was badly underestimated. Since October 7, Israel's population is also fueled by a desire for revenge, by a feeling of anger, if not hatred, toward these "barbarians." This deep resentment will make any rapprochement with Palestinians, though more necessary than ever, extraordinarily difficult, if not impossible, to achieve. Even before October 7, the two-state solution confronted an awkward territorial reality: a Palestinian state, a fine idea, but where, given the annexations performed by Israelis? Today, peace – let us not even speak of reconciliation – seems to be purely utopian. In the mid-1990s, I attended and even moderated some of the secret negotiations of the Oslo Peace Process that took place in Paris at IFRI. The topic discussed there was the future of Jerusalem, while in Rome the issue was the question of the return of Palestinian refugees. During the day, the two delegations disagreed on nearly everything. But in the evening when they left each other, and in the morning when they met again, there existed between Palestinians and Israelis a body language without ambiguity. They were cousins, apart but without anger or hatred. They were conscious of their historical responsibility to bring peace in that part of the world. Of course, Rabin's assassination, Peres's limitations, Netanyahu's (already) cold and shrewd determination were going to put an end to that dream. But what I experienced, albeit briefly, can in retrospect appear as "The Grand Illusion" to plagiarize the title of the movie masterpiece of Jean Renoir – but with a major difference: twenty-five years after the making of that movie (1937), Franco-German reconciliation had become a reality. One would need a miracle, in the biblical sense of the term, to achieve such a result in the context of the Middle East.

Conclusion

"China is becoming a totalitarian state. America is on the brink of chaos. I am investing in Europe and in particular in France." My interlocutor is a rich (very rich) Chinese and American entrepreneur in his sixties who made his fortune in the world of semi-conductors. We had been introduced by a common friend. His openness of tone is both refreshing and surprising. He holds two passports and he speaks with equal pessimism of his two nationalities. One should not base opinions on anecdotes. But his message resonates with my own thinking at the end of this book. (At least this was what I thought before the fateful date of June 9, 2024, when, after a resounding defeat in the elections for the European Parliament, French President Emmanuel Macron took the unfortunate and irresponsible decision to dissolve the National Assembly, opening the door to a parliamentary majority of the National Rally and to political instability in France.) Contrary to what they claim, authoritarian (totalitarian?) regimes are not that efficient. The examples of China with COVID and Russia with Ukraine are ample illustrations of their structural limits. In a world that is ever more complex, the consent of societies is fundamental. Despots are rarely enlightened, especially over a long period of time. Obsessed with their own weaknesses, democracies tend to overestimate their own limitations and to underestimate the structural difficulties of despotic regimes. Obsessed with survival, despotic regimes spend most of their energies in strictly defensive actions. The future is neither in Beijing nor in Moscow. Could it be in New Delhi? It's much too early to say, and, realistically, it is highly unlikely, at least in the mid-term. The hurdles are too high and numerous, from the extreme poverty of so many Indians to the status of women, even if it is slowly, hopefully surely, going in the right direction.

The world has clearly moved East, but not in the direction of despotic regimes. The trend toward totalitarianism kills creativity, dissipates hope, nourishes fear and anger. The evolution of China contains in its very principles the explanation for its ultimate failure. In their aggressive nationalism, the Chinese, after waking up to the world after the death of Mao, have aroused suspicion among the rest of the world, first and foremost among their Asian neighbors. Taiwan possesses an arm of deterrence, much more efficient than the nuclear weapon that is brandished at every opportunity by Putin's Russia: its superiority in the world of semi-conductors.

Despotic regimes are much weaker than they think. Could democracies be stronger than they believe? As far as democracies are concerned, anxiety is legitimate, despair is inappropriate. In geopolitical, political, as well as socio-economic terms, America can rebound, even if its extreme individualism constitutes a handicap, both for itself and for its allies. Americans lack a sense of the collective. "America First," "America Alone" – these slogans hide a deeper personal reality, which means "Me First," "Me Alone."

In a world of rapid and revolutionary economic and technological change – including the rise of AI and the efforts to transition to clean energy – labor anxiety is inevitable. As early as 1997, the brilliant and deliberately controversial historian and essayist Tony Judt warned that "the gap between economic changes and social adjustment had become the critical issue of our time." More than ever, the global economy is undergoing a rapid transformation, creating losers as well as winners. Labor, contrary to capital, cannot move (or not so easily), or at least cannot be separated from its owner. Capital moves around the world at the speed of light. The unanswered social questions do not just wither away. They seek ever more radical answers.

One of the key challenges facing the world is the issue of control, the feeling that you are no longer in charge, that your future is decided by forces that are well beyond your reach. Migration, climate change, and AI have very little in common, except precisely that issue of control. With the rapid influx of migrants, you feel you have lost control on your territory. With the accelerated and dramatic pace of climate change, you sense you are losing control of the planet. And with the revolutionary progress of AI, you think naturally that you have lost control not only of your work, but of the meaning of your life. These three challenges are real and a clear and present danger. But they can also be greeted with a positive energy. The machine pushes you, to give the very best of yourselves. The human eye remains infinitely more precise and nuanced than the very best cameras and photographic instruments in general. It is, at the end of the day, the same with human intelligence, compared with AI.

Climate change, once you have integrated the depth of the existential challenges it represents, can and should also be seen as the opportunity to behave in a responsible way. The idea is not to save the planet *from* humans, as some radical greens seem to favor, but to save the planet *for* humans. Liberating oneself from fossil fuels means taking one's independence from physically and politically polluting energies.

As far as migrants are concerned, they should not be seen just as a threat, but as a gift, a solution. Who would be taking care of the elderly in so many countries of the Western world, including Israel, if foreign workers were not available?

Of course, negative emotions are deeper today than they were in 2009 when I first published my *Geopolitics of Emotion*. With the return of war in Europe, the extension of war in the Middle East, the rise of populism in the world and the partial coming to power of the extreme right in many European countries, including France, how could it be otherwise?

The sense that there is nowhere else to escape to (with the possible exception of Switzerland) unifies the world under the mantle of the tragic. We must nevertheless resist the temptation to see the catastrophic scenario as ineluctable. Even the re-election of Donald Trump in America is not necessarily a tragedy. It will rock the boat of democracy in the United States and beyond. But the democratic model is stronger than its critics believe. It will survive Trump. We are at a turning point, and the democratic West has a compass that the authoritarian regimes do not have: a sense of values. How can the West be tolerant of the "other," while ambitious for itself? This would be exactly the reverse of what we have demonstrated for too long: arrogance toward others, complacency toward ourselves. That is the key question raised in this book. And the battle is not lost.

Beyond the energy of despair, there exists the energy of hope. This is still very present in Kiev, and also evident in the resistance of Iranian and Afghan women. They are giving us lessons in courage and resilience.

Index